COST CONTROL
FOR NONPROFITS
IN CRISIS

ALA Editions purchases fund advocacy, awareness, and accreditation programs for library professionals worldwide.

COST CONTROL
FOR NONPROFITS
IN CRISIS

G. STEVENSON SMITH

AMERICAN LIBRARY ASSOCIATION | CHICAGO 2011

G. Stevenson Smith is the John Massey Endowed Professor of Accounting in the John Massey School of Business at Southeastern Oklahoma State University. He has been on the faculty at universities in Australia, Italy, and New Zealand, and was recently a Fulbright Scholar at the University of Pula in Croatia. Dr. Smith is the author of numerous accounting articles, a coauthor of *Forensic and Investigative Accounting,* 4th edition (CCH 2009), and author of *Managerial Accounting for Libraries and Other Not-for-Profit Organizations* (ALA 2002) and *Accounting for Libraries and Other Not-for-Profit Organizations* (ALA 1999). Prior to entering academia, Dr. Smith was a financial analyst at the Securities and Exchange Commission in Washington, D.C. He received his PhD from the University of Arkansas and is a Certified Public Accountant and a Certified Management Accountant.

Printed in the United States of America

15 14 13 12 11   5 4 3 2 1

While extensive effort has gone into ensuring the reliability of the information in this book, the publisher makes no warranty, express or implied, with respect to the material contained herein.

ISBNs: 978-0-8389-1098-6 (paper); 978-0-8389-9284-5 (PDF). For more information on digital formats, visit the ALA Store at alastore.ala.org and select eEditions.

Library of Congress Cataloging-in-Publication Data
Smith, G. Stevenson.
    Cost control for nonprofits in crisis / G. Stevenson Smith.
        p.   cm.
    Includes bibliographical references and index.
    ISBN 978-0-8389-1098-6 (pbk. : alk. paper) 1. Library finance—United States. 2. Nonprofit organizations—United States—Finance. 3. Libraries—Cost control. 4. Libraries—Cost effectiveness. 5. Nonprofit organizations—Cost control. 6. Nonprofit organizations—Cost effectiveness. 7. Library administration—Decision making. 8. Nonprofit organizations—Management—Decision making. I. Title.
Z683.2.U6S655 2011
025.1′1--dc23   2011025285

Book design in Liberation Serif and DIN by Casey Bayer. Composition by Dianne M. Rooney.
Cover illustration © Vladitto/Shutterstock, Inc.

♾ This paper meets the requirements of ANSI/NISO Z39.48-1992 (Permanence of Paper).

CONTENTS

PREFACE

This book has been written for decision makers in organizations such as libraries, museums, performing arts organizations, country clubs, religious organizations, community organizations, fraternal organizations, labor unions, private foundations, health and welfare organizations, and public broadcasting stations. These organizations are facing funding reductions in today's economic climate. Consequently, they are faced with cutbacks in their services. To help managers cope with these issues, the chapters in this book discuss cost control methods for making better decisions. If the decision to shut down an organization is already made or is imminent, no finance book is going to save the day. But, short of that, these suggestions are made to keep a nonprofit organization from falling into a financial hole.

This book describes the typical daily issues faced by managers regarding the purchase or replacement of assets, budget cutting, and performance evaluation. In addition, strategic organizational problems are covered such as identifying value creation activities and the role of the mission statement in identifying value-added activities. Fraud deterrence is also dealt with in the chapters. The following matrix highlights major topics discussed in this book.

AREA	CHAPTER									
	2	3	4	5	6	7	8	9	10	11
Strategic Planning	X		X	X						
Purchasing Assets			X					X	X	X
Budget Curtailment		X		X						
Replacing Assets								X	X	X
Performance Evaluation					X	X				
Fraud Deterrence							X			

The chapters have been written in a format that helps make the material easy to understand. They have been written so that the manager can quickly review a topic without the need to deal with numerous side bar issues. For a more in-depth look at these financial topics, see G. Stevenson Smith, *Managerial Accounting for Libraries and Other Not-for-Profit Organizations* (ALA 2002), which includes extensive exercises and solutions for each topic in this book.

ONE

INTRODUCTION TO COST CONTROL FOR CULTURAL ORGANIZATIONS

The well-born gentleman avoids the mention of names exactly as he avoids the mention of what things cost; both are an abomination to his soul.

Emily Post, *Etiquette*, 1922

The purpose of this book is to describe decision-making techniques helpful to managers of cultural organizations such as libraries, museums, art councils, civic organizations, theater groups, music societies, professional associations, country clubs, religious organizations, public opera guilds, zoos, community aid organizations, and symphonies. Today, many of these organizations are facing cutbacks in funding that are threatening their existence. For that reason, it is important to determine the most cost-effective method to provide services to their clients or patrons. Yes, Emily, it is necessary to mention "cost."

WHERE'S THE FUNDING?

Forty-one percent of states report declining state funding for U.S. public libraries in fiscal year 2009, according to a survey of the Chief Officers of State Library Agencies (COSLA) conducted by the American Library Association (ALA). Twenty percent of these states anticipate an additional reduction in the current fiscal year.[1]

The techniques outlined here provide the reader with the ability to develop a skill set to identify if costs are being efficiently incurred, monitor financial and nonfinancial performance, cut out "non-value" activities, and develop strategic plans. By using this book, questions such as the following can be answered:

- How do I efficiently plan for the future?
- How do I know if today's decision fits within our mission and vision?
- Can I save money by buying more expensive equipment?
- How do cash flows affect my purchase decisions?

Although budget-setting strategies—such as the give-and-take process—are important, they are not one of the topics discussed in this book. The techniques described in this book allow the manager to identify how to effectively use the budget they are given by making their dollars go as far as possible.

To understand the focus of the book, one must first be aware of differences between managerial decision making and financial accounting as for-profit analytical methods may not be used in a standardized fashion in the nonprofit environment.

MANAGERIAL DECISION MAKING AND COST CONTROL

Managerial decision making is performed on a daily basis by managers in a cultural organization. The decisions made by these directors, department heads, and other supervisors are influenced by managerial cost reports presented to them. Unlike financial accounting statements, managerial reports are not required to follow a prescribed format. Instead, managerial reports provide useful information to the manager so that efficient decisions can be made. These reports may show cost information such as the shelved cost per book or nonfinancial information such as levels of patron satisfaction with a specific program. In most cases, the operation manager will have to request that these reports be prepared as they are not the standardized financial reports usually prepared by an organization's accounting staff.

Unlike financial accounting, where statements are issued at the end of yearly or quarterly periods, managerial reports are prepared as they are needed by managers. The purpose of financial reports is to show what occurred in terms of revenues and expenses in the past year. These reports are not forward looking. With managerial reports, the purpose is to help change or influence decisions occurring in the future. Unlike the aggregated organizational information in financial reports, managerial reports contain specific and detailed information about subunits within the organization. Aggregated financial statement data or budget information cannot take the place of a properly prepared managerial report, nor can the former provide the manager with the information required to make cost-control or strategic decisions. *A manager cannot control his or her organizational costs by using annual financial reports.*

The information in managerial reports goes beyond the reporting found in financial statements. For example, managerial reports can (1) help in analyzing variances from budgeted costs; (2) trace future cost flows, such as maintenance costs, to help in equipment selection decisions; (3) aid in equipment purchasing versus leasing decisions; and (4) determine the break-even level of a service (the point where costs equal support or revenues).

FINANCIAL ACCOUNTING

Financial accounting uses a prescribed set of accounting guidelines in preparing an organization's financial statements. The three financial statements that are prepared under these guidelines are (1) the balance sheet, (2) the income statement, and (3) the statement of cash flows. These financial statements are prepared using prescribed rules called generally accepted accounting principles (GAAP). In the nonprofit area, the Financial Accounting Standards Board (FASB) or the Governmental Accounting Standards Board (GASB) establishes GAAP.[2]

If financial statements are prepared for a nonprofit organization on a basis other than that prescribed by the two boards, and these statements are audited by an independent certified public accountant (CPA), the CPA or auditor will not provide what is known as a "clean" opinion. The CPA's opinion consists of a statement regarding the fairness of presentation in the financial statements. An opinion usually contains boilerplate language about the financial statements, but if material problems occur in the audit, these difficulties need to be reflected in the CPA's opinion. An opinion of this nature is called a qualified opinion, and it is not a clean opinion. Such an opinion would highlight the fact that the financial statements are misleading in some material manner.

In other words, financial accounting places restrictions on the manner in which information can be presented for external reporting. It also can enforce these reporting standards with the auditor's opinion. Of course, there is a reason for this. If prescribed accounting standards are not followed, the consistency and comparability of the financial statements from period to period cannot be assured.

Financial accounting's requirements for following specifically prescribed practices make its practices less concerned with internal cost control and more oriented toward reporting for external groups and stakeholders.

FOR-PROFIT AND NONPROFIT CONTRASTS

In the basic planning for a new project, a comparison is usually made between a periodic series of revenue inflows and expense outflows. The first objective is to ascertain, as best as possible, if the cash inflows from the activities will exceed the outflows. The second objective, if several choices are available, is to select the project with the highest net inflow. Generally, if projected cash inflows exceed outflows on a project, the decision criteria will allow for acceptance of the project. The greater profit premise is basic to the managerial analysis that is performed in a *for-profit* context.

In nonprofit organizations, earning a profit has limited application. Measures of nonprofit success are not marked by earning the highest monetary profit. In most nonprofit operations, managerial emphasis is placed on the level of services provided to patrons. If costs are not recovered, the service may be provided anyway and funded from other sources such as donations or grants. A nonprofit organization's operations may generate cash outflows which always exceed cash revenue inflows. For example, the operating costs of zoological or botanical parks have always exceeded any fee revenues charged to the users of these parks. Therefore, the techniques of for-profit analysis needed to be changed if they are used in a nonprofit context.

Not using profit generation as a measure of success indicates that decision making in a nonprofit organization is at variance with decision making in a for-profit company. As an example, consider depreciation expense in for-profit and nonprofit contexts. Depreciation expense is an accounting allocation where the purchase price of an asset with a life of more than one year is assigned to the time periods over which the asset is used. This allocation procedure assigns the asset's purchase price in a "reasonable" manner to the time periods of estimated asset use, but no cash outflows arise from this allocation procedure. The only cash outflow that might have occurred took place when the asset was originally purchased.

Depreciation expense in a for-profit context is important because it reduces the taxes that a corporation pays; depreciation is a tax-deductible expense. Without a reduction of revenues from depreciation expenses, higher taxes result in larger cash outflows to the Internal Revenue Service. Therefore, depreciation expenses are important in making managerial decisions in a for-profit business. But, in organizations that do not pay taxes, the importance of depreciation expense to decision making is reduced. In fact, recording depreciation may be a nuisance to managerial decision makers because noncash depreciation expense deductions must be added back to determine the total cash flowing into an organization. The managerial importance of depreciation expense in a nonprofit context is restricted to providing an indication as to the extent to which facilities' usefulness has vanished over the years. Here, the sum of all the recorded depreciation provides an indirect insight into the usefulness of an organization's infrastructure.

For a nonprofit organization, a more important asset question than accumulating depreciation is: "How well have the assets been maintained?" For any organization, but especially for a nonprofit entity, the amount spent to maintain assets is more pertinent than knowing the amount of accumulated depreciation of a specific asset. The level of normal preventive maintenance on an asset can be established by manufacturer's guidelines within a fairly specific range. If these preventive maintenance procedures are not followed, the expected life of the asset is reduced prematurely. It is fairly common to see public infrastructures literally collapsing because of curtailed maintenance. In these instances, maintenance was stopped in an attempt to save budget dollars. Without proper maintenance of facilities, public funds in excess of initial projections will have to be used to replace prematurely deteriorated facilities or to fund above-normal, emergency maintenance repairs. Even though maintenance expenditure information is not specifically reported in the financial statements, it can be recorded in managerial reports. Information about the amount of deferred maintenance can be more important to a nonprofit manager than the annual depreciation expense recorded. This illustrates another basic difference between managerial decision making in for-profit and nonprofit organizations.

Care should be taken to separate the practices used in for-profit organizations from those used in nonprofit organizations. The approach taken in this book is to explain the practices of nonprofit managerial decision making.

WHO'S YOUR AGENT?

A primary nonprofit managerial accounting objective is to provide the greatest amount of cost-efficient services to the largest number of people. The best nonprofit financial techniques are used to achieve this objective. Often, however, when the final course of action is chosen, it may be different than the recommended solution arrived at through the use of financial analysis. Why does this occur?

Financial analysis uses the best analytical techniques for arriving at a managerial decision, but it does not incorporate political and behavioral factors that are very real influences in nonprofit organizations. So, it is necessary for analytical methods to consider political and behavioral factors as they affect managerial decision making. Agency theory is used to describe these effects on managerial decision making.[3]

The basic premise in agency theory is that someone other than the owner of the organization (the agent) manages the organization. In nonprofit organizations, this manager is the director, and the owners are either the groups that provide monetary resources or, in some cases, the groups that are receiving services. In a nonprofit, an agency relationship exists between the director and the board, the director and the governmental entities providing funding, and the director and the service groups. Agency theory relationships are present any time decision-making authority has been delegated to a subordinate, such as the director or other manager. A basic assumption of agency theory is that the managers are out to maximize benefits to themselves. The agent is chiefly concerned with satisfying his or her own self-interests without regard to the needs of the owners or the organization. Agency theory forms the basis for changing those relationships from self-interest to one which optimizes the welfare of the organization and the groups it serves.

Under agency theory, methods are used that attempt to overcome the self-interest or opportunism of the managers. Opportunism occurs when a manager selects solutions to a problem that are in the best interests of that manager but not necessarily in the best interests of the organization or the groups the manager serves. For example, the best solution for a manager may mean exercising the least amount of effort regardless of the outcome.

The lack of congruence between the manager's goal and the service goals of the organization should be a concern in nonprofit management.

> ## SO WHAT?
>
> As the administrator of a Fannie Mae grant for community organizations serving low-income clients, the author was confronted with two administrators who were not interested in receiving additional funding that accompanied consulting services to increase the delivery effectiveness of their services. The reason: "We are only interested in getting next year's grant monies. This doesn't help."

Personal ambition or the rewards of prestige that come from a position may be factors in a manager's decision-making process that determine whether he or she will accept higher levels of career risk in order to provide better services.

A great deal of the analysis used by managers is based on estimates, and estimates are often biased because of a managerial manipulation of information. The manager, in direct control of an operation, usually is assumed to have the best information about its operation. Therefore, it may be difficult for others to determine if an estimate is unbiased or if it is biased to further the manager's interests.

A manager may be asked to make estimates of such things as the time it takes to finish a project, personnel requirements, or the amount of use a new service will receive once it is offered. The estimate that is received from the manager is used to prepare an internal report, to evaluate the feasibility of a project, or to develop a grant proposal. Any bias introduced into the manager's estimate is often difficult to detect because evaluative information is only received after the action has been implemented. Therefore, the accuracy of managerial estimates can be determined only on the basis of historically collected information. Agency theory is directed at correcting the causes of these managerial contrivances.

> ## WHAT ABOUT . . . NO HOMEWORK FOR THE TEACHER
>
> A high school teacher provides a brief explanation of one math problem in the classroom, and then hands out exercises for the students to work for the rest of the class period. While the students are working, the teacher grades papers or reads. Is the teacher using instructional time to grade papers so that she does not have to work on them in the evening? Does the teacher realize the students' attention spans are so short that making a long presentation would be futile? Is this an example of slacking or not?

As an example, assume a director is on an upward career path. In accepting a new position, this person is mainly concerned with how personal accomplishments in the new job will have an impact on his or her next job. For a manager, establishing a track record of accomplishments is important. This track record is oriented toward the short term (three years). The director will seek out projects that contribute positively to his or her three-year record of performance. Some of these decisions may not be in the best interests of the nonprofit organization. For example, the director might install computers for the public to use in order to list a computer initiative on her vita. In implementing this initiative, the cheapest computers are purchased, with little technical support, no maintenance agreement, and hardly any software. In this example, the computers will have to be completely discarded within a four-year period, after providing little public service. The limited four-year life of these computers is not important to the manager because he or she is likely to have found another better-paying job before the limitations of the initiative become apparent. Additionally, if the cheapest computers are purchased, funds may be left over so that the director can start another "initiative" that will make his or her résumé even more impressive. Agency theory is concerned with establishing contractual relationships to prevent this type of behavior from occurring.

One particularly difficult nonprofit managerial problem is how to monitor an individual's performance to prevent nonproductive behaviors. In a for-profit organization, a worker's profit performance can be easily seen and evaluated, but in most nonprofit organizations, it is particularly difficult to evaluate performance. How can a nonprofit organization determine if the director is not interested in an upward career path but instead is more interested in expending a minimum amount of effort?

These examples illustrate the special problems that may arise when traditional managerial methods are introduced into the nonprofit organization. Nonprofit organizations have been criticized for not adopting the modem methods of business; however, these methods may not have been properly modified for the context of the nonprofit organization, and do not take into consideration the managerial behavioral characteristics described in agency theory. It is possible to correct for this behavior in several ways, as is explained later.

WHAT IS NONPROFIT COST MANAGEMENT?

With the differences between nonprofit and for-profit entities in mind, what is nonprofit cost management? Nonprofit cost management adapts the techniques of for-profit analysis to a nonprofit environment to control operating costs. It adapts the best analytical techniques in the corporate world to the special environment of nonprofit organizations.

The major emphasis in business is for profits to exceed costs by as much as possible. In nonprofit managerial accounting, cost containment is important if the nonprofit organization is to remain viable so that quality services can be provided to patrons. Cost performance needs to be evaluated to determine how efficiently services are being provided. Without cost control, the resource base within the organization erodes to a level that results in the organization's service activities deteriorating or even being discontinued. Facilities are run down. Staff is let go. And the only way the organization can continue is with a severe curtailment in its services or quality. Here, we are looking for a way around that outcome. These methods use both short-term crisis control and long-term goals. Yet, if your nonprofit organization is faced with shutting its doors, there is little anyone can do for you at that point.

> ### HOW MUCH DOES IT COST?
>
> Children's Museum of Wilmington Executive Director Mark Kesling said, "We think we have great value here and a lot to offer. When we first opened we really did take a shot in the dark as to what it would take to operate this new building and this new facility and so we needed to make this adjustment, based on what it really does cost for us to do this."[4]

WHO WILL BENEFIT FROM THIS BOOK?

Cost control, project evaluation, and strategic planning are the primary topics in this book. Managers in a nonprofit organization who are required to control costs or make choices between service levels as budgets are curtailed will find this book useful. Nonprofit boards interested in controlling costs can use the illustrations in this book to request that similar reports be prepared within their organizations. In a period of budget reductions, downsizing, and cost curtailment, the importance of an efficient and cost-effective organization needs to be emphasized. Therefore, it is important to be familiar with the techniques described in this book. The book describes methods that allow nonprofit managers to determine whether the organization's mission is being efficiently accomplished. Readers who are likely to benefit from the material in this book are those individuals who have operating responsibility within a nonprofit organization.

SUMMARY

The purpose of this book is to illustrate to those who have operating responsibility within a nonprofit organization that there are techniques for guiding them as they evaluate projects and make managerial decisions.

Further, managerial nonprofit decision making cannot unhesitatingly adopt the techniques used by for-profit organizations. A director should not expect to make managerial decisions based on the annual financial statements and reports prepared for external stakeholder's use. Further, budgets provide the rules on spending levels and variances from approved dollar amounts. These budgets do not provide for the underlying managerial analysis of how much should be provided in the first place. . . . what is the cost of efficient operations. They, too, can be used for budget line cost control, but they do not provide the means to arrive at cost efficient operations.

NOTES

1. "State Funding for Many Public Libraries on Decline," American Library Association Press Release, February 10, 2009, www.ala.org/ala/newspresscenter/news/pressreleases2009/february2009/orscosla.cfm.

2. The Governmental Accounting Standards Board (GASB) sets accounting standards for state and local governments, and the Financial Accounting Standards Board (FASB) sets accounting standards for business organizations. The organizations set standards with the issuance of statements and with audit guides. When a library is part of a state and local government, its financial statements are not prepared separately from those of the state and local government, and the library is considered to be part of the state or government organization. Usually, the only separate financial reports this type of library receives are related to budgetary data. If a library is not considered to be part of a government organization, its financial statements must be prepared using a different method of accounting than used by the state and local government.

3. For a basic introduction to agency theory, read D. B. Thornton, "A Look at Agency Theory for the Novice: Part 1," *CA Magazine* (November 1984), 90–97; and D. B. Thornton, "A Look at Agency Theory for the Novice: Part II," *CA Magazine* (January 1985), 93–100.

4. "Children's Museum Price Increase Upsets Parents," wwaytv3.com, February 8, 2007, www.wwaytv3.com/node/231/.

TWO

USING THE VALUE CHAIN FOR STRATEGIC ANALYSIS

If things are not going well with you, begin your effort at correcting the situation by carefully examining the service you are rendering, and especially the spirit in which you are rendering it.

Roger Babson

Michael Porter (1985) described the concept of the value chain.[1] The value chain links the activities of an organization together to help the organization identify the activities it performs to create value for its patrons, clients, or customers. The value chain is used to chart the organizational processes that create value for stakeholders. The links begin with "raw materials" and end with the valued "product" that the client or customer receives. The separation of activities into the value chain eventually allows for a clear view of the organization's cost structure and how the expending of those costs is contributing to activities that create value for the organization. For a university, the beginning of the value chain or its "raw materials" starts with the new students entering college as freshman. The work that lies ahead for the university to create value for its patrons is dependent on the abilities of the entering freshmen. If they have been well-prepared, the university's job becomes easier. If they are unprepared, the university may find it necessary to have a sequence of remedial courses in order to get these students ready to take college courses. Consequently, it is necessary for the university to incur educational costs that should have been incurred by the high schools these students attended. Regardless, the value chain for the university begins outside its campus and ends with a "product" that is a graduate of the university.

What is the final product of a corporate research library? The final product from the research library is related to the research reports the library supported. What is the final product from a museum? The final product is the exhibits displayed. What is the final product from a civic organization? The services provided to patrons.

The amount by which revenues exceed costs (i.e., profits) is not a method for judging such nonprofit organizations (NP), but the value created for their customers or patrons is a method that can be used to judge their performance.

A generalized nonprofit value chain is illustrated in figure 2.1. Each NP should have a strong understanding of how they create value for the users of their services.

The value chain in figure 2.1 includes activities that occur both inside and outside the organization's physical boundaries. These activities move from the left to the right in the illustration. The external suppliers as well as final outcomes exist beyond the organizational boundaries, but they are still part of the NP's value chain. An organizational objective is to have suppliers providing services or resources in a manner that reduces organizational costs or at least does not increase the costs of operations. These external suppliers are usually considered to be suppliers of material used in operating the nonprofit organization. Yet, these suppliers can also be donors or grantors of funding. For this reason, suppliers should be considered to be anyone or any organization contributing resources to the NP and not just supply vendors. All suppliers bring their own overhead costs as they provide resources to the organization.

For example, software suppliers may sell software packages that need to be continually updated. The objective of the software seller may be to market a software package as early as possible in order to capture a large market share. Consequently, the labor cost related to

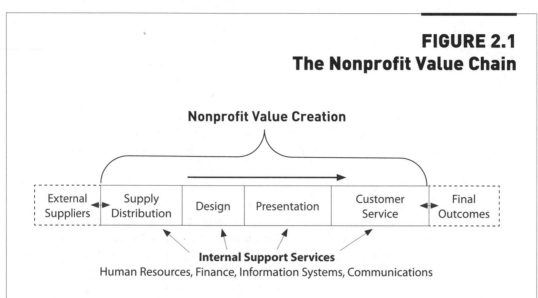

FIGURE 2.1
The Nonprofit Value Chain

Nonprofit Value Creation

| External Suppliers | Supply Distribution | Design | Presentation | Customer Service | Final Outcomes |

Internal Support Services
Human Resources, Finance, Information Systems, Communications

Typical Internal Value Creation Activities

1. *Supply:* Receiving/unpacking, internal distribution of supplies, and inventory management. Distributing funding resources within the organization.
2. *Design:* Strategic planning, training, screening employees, facility maintenance, and continuing professional development
3. *Presentation:* Tactical planning, promotion, technical assistance, building security and theft.
4. *Customer Service:* Establishing rapport with customers or clients, handling inquiries or complaints, and providing *actual* helpfulness in meeting the service needs of the client.

Typical External Contributions to the Value Chain

1. *External Suppliers:* The efficiency of these suppliers in providing resources affects the organization's value creation abilities.
2. *Final Outcomes:* These outcomes are what are internalized by the individuals who use the nonprofit's services. The perspective developed by these user groups may or may not be what was intended by the nonprofit organization.

making the updates along with downtime costs are passed on to the NP from the software manufacturer. This is an example of outside overhead costs being passed downstream as well as a way in which value creation becomes curtailed due to a reduction in resources.

Even funding provided to an NP comes with its own costs. For public funds, these costs may be related to the hours needed to prepare fund-use reports, provide seminars to funding agencies, special meetings, and attendance at agency briefing sessions. For donor funding, the costs may be more subtle but nonetheless required for the continuation of additional support from this donor. Such donor-related costs may involve providing special lectures, additional formal evening gatherings at the NP's facilities, and changes in the schedule of exhibits. All these costs can be considered to be overhead associated with the receipt of resources given to the NP, and again a possible distraction from providing patron services.

As the NP meets the requirements and needs of these suppliers using its finite resources, the result can be a reduction in the overall ability of the organization to meet its core function of providing public services. But, in order to make that statement, the NP needs to have identified its core functions. Depending on the NP, those core functions involve activities such as providing research support, developing new exhibits, financial aid for low income clients, quality reviews of service activities, expanding outreach to the public, and updating of databases. Whether resources are provided by a donor or purchased, they all come with a cost that needs to be explicitly identified and compared with the funding provided to the NP. In some cases the costs may outweigh the benefits received. In those cases, such funding reduces the ability of the organization to create its core values and service its clients.

Figure 2.1 shows the internal processes in the value chain as supply, design, presentation and customer service. In a manufacturing firm, these processes would be related to the production of products. Here, supply refers to internal distribution of resources to the NP's departments and personnel. The distribution can be done by the personnel who receive the supplies and agency funding or by an NP director who may distribute discretionary donor funds. Supply is not confined to one department in the NP's organizational structure such as a receiving department. Supply relates to managers who have the authority to distribute incoming resources. Similarly design refers to long-range activities that contribute to value creation in the organization. Again these functions are not restricted to one specific department, but all departments involved in these activities need to be closely coordinated. Design is composed of developing the strategic organizational processes including recruitment, professional development, planning, budgeting, developing performance evaluation standards, mission statement creation, and identification of objectives to meet the organizational mission. Presentation is related to the actual implementation of short-range processes used to satisfy strategic performance goals. It is called "presentation" because these are the activities that are apparent to those who use the NP's services. Value creation in the presentation stage are represented by good building security, cleanliness of the facility, effectiveness of programs presented to the public, strong technical abilities of service personnel, organizational coordination used to meet strategic objectives, successful program outcomes, and well-maintained and technological up-to-date equipment. Again, the activities in presentation need to be coordinated, but they do not have to occur in one department as in a traditional organization. The input processes used in the presentation stage are tangible and can be measured. Their effects translate into customer service and final outcomes in the value chain. Customer service relates to how customers or clients view and react to the NP's presentation processes. Building rapport with an NP's service group occurs at this point in the value chain. For example, the manner in which inquiries and complaints are handled is an important part of the customer service mission. Customer service allows an NP to build a supportive relationship with their customers based on the customer-perceived usefulness of the provided services and the manner in which those services are provided to the service group.

Presentation inputs provide the potential for creating a perspective of usefulness, but the customer must also believe they are receiving a worthwhile benefit. The presentation is creating value for the organization if the customer believes service *value* is being created for *them.* Final outcomes are internalized by the individuals who use the nonprofit's services. The perspective developed by these user groups may or may not be what was intended by the nonprofit organization. These user groups can be the clients served by the NP, the NP's donors, or the agencies that provide financial support. The effects of these views have the potential to increase or decrease future support provided to the NP.

The four internal-value creation processes are based on the core competencies found within an NP. These activities are central to the successful operation of an NP, but there are also activities that support those core processes. These functions are shown in figure 2.1 as internal support services. They are represented by departments such as human resources, finance, information systems, and communications. These support activities are needed by the NP organization, but they are not the reason an NP is in existence. Therefore, these support functions should be scrutinized to determine if their costs can be reduced. For-profit organizations have faced the same issue and they have responded by outsourcing many of their support functions without any loss in the quality of their products or services.

VALUE CREATION IN THE ORGANIZATION: DOES IT WORK?

Every NP wants to create value for its service group, but it seems that many auxiliary issues arise that create non-value activities. Non-value activities are those organizational functions that do not increase service value to the NP's patrons. Governmental and nonprofit organizations have a tendency to expand their non-value activities. The consequence is that these functions have the potential to override the organization's ability to provide its core services. For example, the traditional organization chart of an NP is not usually organized around the value creating activities outlined in figure 2.1. Instead the organization is organized in a very traditional manner, and managerial efforts are made to squeeze value from a traditional organization hierarchy such as the one illustrated in figure 2.2.

For the medium-sized library in figure 2.2, various directors are responsible for evaluating the functions of the departments under their responsibility. They, too, are being evaluated with final authority resting with the library board or other such group. These activities are creating internal value among departments, but where are the interactions with the organization's service group (i.e., its patrons, clients, or customers) taking place? Those services are directly provided within the lowest levels of the organizational chart. For this library they are provided through Adult Circulation, Children's Library, Special Collections, the Extension Department (Branches, Hospital Library, and Bookmobile) and Reference. In the nonprofit value chain, this is where the processes of presentation, customer service, final outcomes and some design processes are located. These departments are where the core values are provided to patrons.

Although the example in figure 2.2 represents a library, the situation is similar for most NP organizations. In figure 2.2, the patron value-creating processes occur in the lowest rungs of the organization's hierarchy; while value creation related to indirect support functions such as ordering, cataloging, asset maintenance, purchasing, accounting, and administrative functions occur in the highest rungs of the organization chart. The latter grouping is where the largest section of organizational operating cost is expended in the traditional organization.

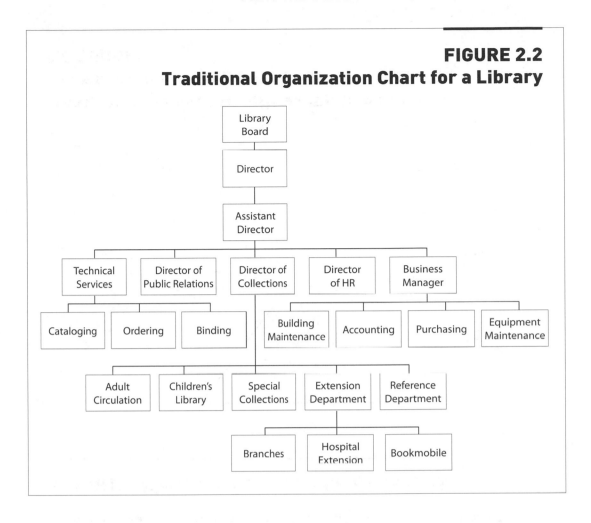

FIGURE 2.2
Traditional Organization Chart for a Library

For this reason, it can be seen that indirect value creation costs are the major expenditures in the traditional organization. When cost control is necessary, these are the costs that need to be curtailed—not the costs related to patron services.

Each organization's core value creation processes need indirect support, but the question becomes one of determining what percentage of total expenditures should be made up of indirect costs. Within government and NPs, support processes tend to become a natural end in themselves while the provision of actual customer or patron services turns into a secondary activity. Support functions need to be annually reviewed to determine if they have reached an *unbalanced value point* within the organization. All organizations tend toward such a point of imbalance. Once the organization reaches value imbalance, it needs to be determined how to go back to a balance between value creation and support activities. Figure 2.3 illustrates an NP whose cost structure is out of balance because its administrative support expenditures are outweighing its client service costs. Steps to rebalance the organization may require the outsourcing of non-value-creating support activities such as cataloging or accounting, or rebalancing administrative structure to ensure the largest share of expenditures are made in the client service area.

The value chain and organizational hierarchy structures tend not to work together to achieve the organization's objectives. As long as there is a separation between the two systems, it will result in either a decrease in value creation or value creation only at a higher cost to the organization. Even so, the traditional hierarchical organization continues to dominate management structures in NPs.

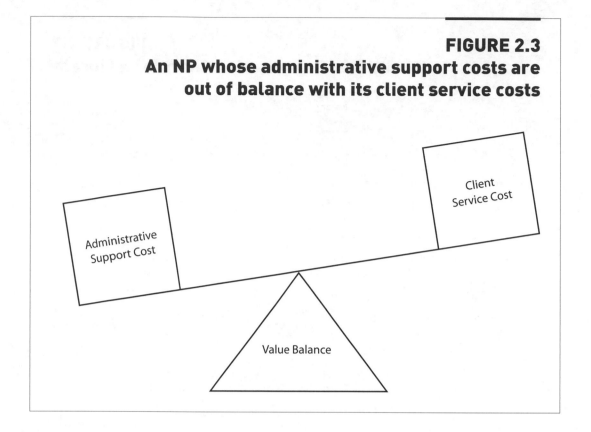

FIGURE 2.3
An NP whose administrative support costs are out of balance with its client service costs

EVERYONE WANTS TO BE AN ADMINISTRATOR

New evidence suggests that a growing percentage of public school funds are being spent on district administration rather than on teaching. According to Standard & Poor's, the private company hired by the state to analyze school data from Michigan public schools and public school academies, central administration costs have risen more than twice as fast as instructional expenses, including teacher salaries, over the past three years.[2]

. . . assumes universities apply public funding to their stated goals of educating students and conducting research, which is not always the case. A recent audit of UNC-Chapel Hill found millions in potential savings by reducing spending on administrative costs, which have accelerated at a greater rate than spending on academics.[3]

STEPPING BEYOND THE TRADITIONAL ORGANIZATIONAL CHART TO CREATE VALUE

Once it is recognized there is a difference between value creation and traditional management control systems, the question needs to be asked if there is a way for these two systems to work together or overlap one another.

The first step in trying to make the traditional organization increase its value output is to determine its unbalance value point status. This review is done by looking at an up-to-date organization chart and identifying each unit in the chart that creates direct value for customers or clients. The percentage expenditure mixture needs to be estimated. If the non-value-creating part of the organization is 60 percent or more of its expenditures, the

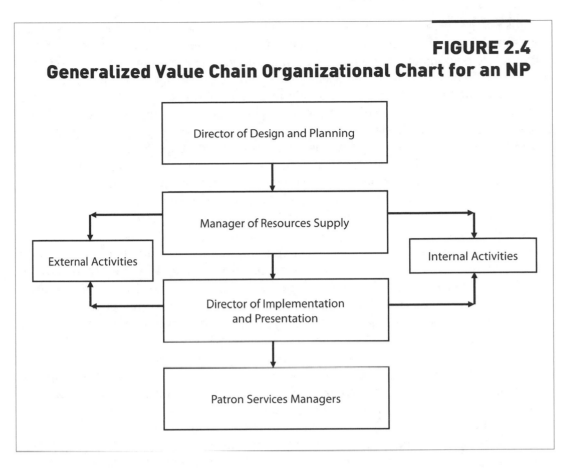

FIGURE 2.4

Generalized Value Chain Organizational Chart for an NP

organization is in an unbalanced state and such an organization is not going to be able to deliver satisfactory services to its service groups. At a minimum, the value creation activities need to include more than 50 percent of all expenditures in a service organization—that is, 60 to 70 percent of organizational expenditures.

Traditional organizations attempt to create value with ad hoc management groups. For example, to increase the value creation activities in such organizations ad hoc committees are formed. These committees are used to operate outside the traditional organization lines of authority to attempt to create value. The committees formed under Total Quality Management guidelines are examples of such a structure. Unfortunately, the lines of authority and responsibility follow the lines in the organization chart, and therefore the work of these committees is restricted to limited areas, and in many cases their recommendations are ignored. Therefore, their value creating ability is generally limited or nonexistent.

There may be other ways to view the NP that go beyond the traditional organizational chart. For example, depending on the NP, it may be able to base its organizational chart and the lines of organizational authority around the value chain rather than a functionally based departmental structure (e.g., accounting, business department, etc.). Figure 2.4 is an example of such a structure.

Figure 2.4 illustrates a generalized value chain organizational chart. The large numbers of departments and divisions in figure 2.2, the traditional organizational chart for a library, have been collapsed into a series of units related to the core values created by the NP. In figure 2.4, the departments correspond more closely with the value creating activities that are found in the value chain in figure 2.1. These activities begin with the design and planning process. The director of design and planning is responsible for overseeing the daily activities of the organization as well as strategic planning. In order to be able to adequately focus on those daily operations, non-value-adding activities of the organization are outsourced. For example, cataloging, accounting, certain routine activities in human resources, binding, building and equipment maintenance are prime candidates for outsourcing. Other activities would need to be eliminated. The operations within a separate public relations department could be eliminated. With training, public relations could become a natural function of many employees' jobs just as quality control has become part of many employees' jobs in a production facility. Purchasing is moved into manager of resources supply. The manager of this unit is responsible for providing the materials needed to implement the strategic plans developed in conjunction with the director of design and planning or providing information as to the reason a proposed plan cannot be implemented. Obviously, the ability to implement plans needs to be evaluated by these two units *before* they are completed.

The various library departments such as Children's Library and Adult Circulation are collapsed into the unit under the director of implementation and presentation. There are both internal and external value-adding activities under the responsibility of the director of implementation and presentation and manager of resource supply. The external activities are what are seen and/or used by the NP's patrons. The internal activities, such as training, are viewed by the employees who are working to provide services (presentation) to these patrons. Patron services managers are working to ensure the services provided to patrons are furnished in a professional manner. They are not responsible for assessing the quality of the services provided. Such an assessment must be done by an independent entity separate from the services manager's area of authority to ensure an independent assessment is completed.

The driver behind such an organization chart is value creation based on the organization's core activities—that is, what it does best. Another purpose of such an organizational chart is to keep the subdivisions within the organization focused on value creation rather than on keeping their "turf" intact. Can a traditional organizational chart be changed into a value creating organizational chart? For many organizations the answer is "no" and these organizations must continue to try to create value for their patrons under the authorizations in a traditional organizational chart.

CAN IT BE DONE?

Vera Institute of Justice is a research and policy-developing NP. Its mission is to make the U.S. justice system more humane. In the mid-1990s, Vera reorganized itself around its value chain. The elements in its value chain were identified around Vera's research expertise as:

1. Research to evaluate new and ongoing projects
2. Planning to develop new programs
3. Demonstration by beginning demo projects
4. Spinoffs for implementing successful demonstration projects within another NP or government agency

The new organizational network helps create significant more NP value through the development of a series of more successful projects.[4]

WHAT STOPS VALUE CREATING ORGANIZATIONAL CHARTS FROM BEING USED?

Changing a traditional organization to a value-based organization requires a deep revision that goes down to the basic foundation of the NP. It needs to be remembered that the concept of the traditional organizational chart developed as small manufacturing firms grew into diverse enterprises. The organizational chart was used to control the diverse branches of these larger organizations. Later, the chart was adapted to NP organizations. These charts were developed when the idea of value-adding activities was not yet conceived. The charts are from a time when outsourcing consisted of using a local machinist shop for producing automobile components and not outsourcing to another country half way around the world. The chart was developed when using overnight secretarial services in China to complete documents for use the next morning in the U.S. was inconceivable or when technological value creation for the U.S. market occurred in the U.S., not in India. Even though it is a different world today, the traditional organizational chart based on competing departments dominates operational manager's thinking. Therefore, the effort to change to a value-based organizational chart is not readily acceptable.

Another reason for not changing to a value-based chart may be related to legal requirements or politically mandated rules to maintain certain separate departments within an NP's organizational structure. This is especially true for government-based NPs. Nongovernment NPs have the ability to change to a value-based approach with less difficulty.

SUMMARY

The traditional organization chart shows the authority relationships among job holders, and job holders are concerned with supporting upper-level authority holders in order to be successful in their jobs. Consequently, in order to make the organizational authority chart work, it is necessary to perform activities that do not necessarily add value to the patron services provided by the NP. The traditional organizational chart shows the chain of command, but not necessarily how value is created in the organization. The value chain does show how activities contribute to providing valued service to patrons. Although there may be an overlap in the two, there is no guarantee that they overlap each other in any manner. Furthermore, there is a natural tendency in service organizations to develop a high level of supporting activities and unintentionally minimize the level of direct service provided to its patrons. The next chapter discusses how to eliminate non-value-added activities and reduce the operating costs for NP organizations as they struggle to maintain their service levels in an era of diminishing funding support.

NOTES

1. Michael E. Porter, *Competitive Advantage: Creating and Sustaining Superior Performance* (New York: Free Press, 1985).

2. "Michigan Administrative Expenses Top $1.4 Billion," *Education Report*, May 30, 2002, www.educationreport.org/pubs/mer/article.aspx?id=4366.

3. "College Costs: Hold Constitution's Principle on Tuition," *Reflector.com*, November 25, 2009, www.reflector.com/opinion/college-costs-hold-constitutions-principle-on-tuition-976820.html.

4. "Effective Capacity Building in Nonprofit Organizations," *Venture Philanthropy Partners*, 2001.

THREE

THE 10 PERCENT SOLUTION

*"I'm living so far beyond my income that we may almost
be said to be living apart."*

E. E. Cummings,
The Unbearable Bassington

Chapter 2 described the value chain and how managers need to consider whether it is possible to manage an NP with a focus on patron value creation. There are many organizational roadblocks preventing managers from being able to implement value-creating decisions within their NP. One of them is managerial unfamiliarity with the activities in the organization that directly create costs. Another is a financial reporting system that makes it difficult to identify the relationship between costs and activities. Both of these problems will be dealt with in this chapter as well as the following two chapters.

When managers are faced with a decrease in budget funding, it is difficult for them to see how they can continue to focus on value-creating activities. When a manager is faced with a 10 percent across-the-board budget cut, it means every line item needs to be cut by the same 10 percent. This is the 10 percent solution. . . . or 5 percent solution depending on the level of budget reduction required. The budget reports presented to the manager show expenditures by department and expenditure item. Thus, the easiest choice is to cut back evenly on every expenditure item. Yet, even in this decision-making environment, it is still possible to identify and cut the costs of activities in the organization that do not create direct patron value.

When across-the-board budget cuts of 5 to 10 percent are required, it means those who impose cuts have little understanding of what actually occurs within the organization. With across-the-board cuts, the cost of every organization activity must be reduced by the same percentage. In Chapter 2, it was pointed out that not all NP operations contribute to value creation equally. Therefore, when it is necessary to cut costs, a better decision is to cut non-value-creating activities more than those that create value. In order to make such a decision, it is necessary to have the strength of political conviction that this is the best choice for the organization's service population and then know which activities contribute the greatest or least value to the organization. Without having developed the groundwork for value-based decisions, managers must fall back on the 10 percent solution to reducing their budgets as there is no alternative.

The groundwork for selective budget reduction begins with identifying NP activities and determining the contribution they make to value creation. The managerial approach to make such choices begins with implementing activity-based management (ABM).

EVERYONE MUST SUFFER EQUALLY . . . JUST BECAUSE

RIVERSIDE: County recommends 10 percent budget cuts

No department exempt

RIVERSIDE—County supervisors on Tuesday accepted recommendations that all departments plan 10 percent budget cuts and they affirmed that dark days lay ahead. [1]

Like all state agencies, the Georgia Department of Natural Resources has been ordered to cut at least 6 percent from its budget, and possibly as much as 10 percent.

"The DNR has six divisions, but two of them, Wildlife Resources and State Parks, are involved in land management and are very personnel-heavy," said DNR spokeswoman Beth Brown. "The only way to achieve the cuts we need is to close facilities."[2]

ACTIVITY-BASED MANAGEMENT

Activity-based management (ABM) begins with an analysis of the activities occurring in an NP. Activities are repetitive actions that are performed by specialized organizational groups to achieve the mission and goals of the NP. It is necessary to determine how these activities drive up the operating costs of the organization, and then identify those cost drivers that are creating organizational value. If an activity is a cost driver but does not directly contribute to creating organizational value, it should be considered for elimination when budget reductions are required. On the other hand, every effort should be expended to maintain those cost-driving activities that contribute to organizational value.

Under traditional organizational management, little emphasis is directed at identifying activities performed; emphasis is placed on the dollar level of resources consumed, for example, the human resources budget, the supplies budget, or the travel and training budget. ABM begins with identifying activities followed by cost assignment, rather than emphasizing departmental expenditure budgets.

Activities can be divided into a specific series of tasks required to complete a function. For example, the acquisition of library materials under an acquisitions department includes tasks such as ordering and receiving. The task of receiving library materials can be further separated into unpacking books, matching invoices with materials, matching purchase orders with invoices, returning unordered or damaged materials, corresponding with vendors, recording cancellations, reviewing standing orders, and distributing books to proper work areas for further processing and shelving. These are the activities that drive the direct costs in acquisitions. When the activities in a department are identified, it starts to become clear to managers how reducing activities may reduce costs.

THE 21.4 PERCENT SOLUTION

Phoenix Public Library Faces 21.4 Percent Budget Cut; Six of 15 Branches Would Close

At the main Burton Barr Library, five staffers would be laid off, reducing in-person and remote reference and other service assistance. Friday service would be cut at all branches, thus reducing 10.8 positions. And the six closed branches would mean that 57.7 positions would be lost.

The sixth-largest city in the country, at about 1.5 million, sprawling Phoenix already has relatively few library locations for a city of its size; the library would be challenged to find new ways to provide service to areas where branches were closed.[3]

IDENTIFYING ACTIVITIES

As an example of ABM, consider the Technical Services Department in the Walter Hoosier Library, a medium-sized city library. The monthly budget for the direct activities of technical services is $27,980. The $27,980 is the budget expenditure appearing on the Hoosier Library's Budget as the monthly expenditure for Technical Services. Assume the Head of Technical Services, Sarah Richards, is faced with a 5 percent budget reduction ($1,399 per month or $16,788 annually). Obviously, she needs more information than is available from the Hoosier's budget report to implement this reduction.

Sarah wants to determine how to cut the Technical Services budget and still maintain the services to other library departments and patrons. She is aware that if the Hoosier's entire budget is cut, book purchases will drop and that would automatically decrease technical service costs, but she is uncertain as to which departmental costs will drop.

To start the process, Sarah developed a list of service activities occurring in the department:

- Bibliographic checking
- Book distribution
- Cataloging
- Withdrawal of materials
- Online catalog maintenance
- Shelf list maintenance

The next step is to assign costs to these activities. Cost assignment ties a direct cost to the activity that causes the costs to increase (i.e., cost drivers). In this example, increases in the number of books purchased drive up bibliographic checking costs. The number of books purchased also drives the costs of distribution, cataloging, and online catalog maintenance. Withdrawal of materials may be a function of the space available and number of items ordered. Self list maintenance is done based on passage of time and departmental policies.

Other costs of running the department would not change if the number of books requested or ordered increased or decreased. These are the salary cost of personnel working in Technical Services. The department head's salary does not change based on changes in orders nor do the salaries of the other personnel working in the department. The total salaries paid out are 41 percent of her budget. In addition, there are three student workers in the library whose salaries are equal to $1,175 which raises salaries paid in the department to 45 percent of the budget. The only way these costs can be reduced during budget cutbacks is by releasing employees or dropping full-time employees to a part-time status, usually without benefits.

Sarah is fairly certain budget reductions can be made without reducing personnel. In order to better understand cost incurrence patterns in the department, she had a monthly cost report prepared. It is shown in figure 3.1. Figure 3.1 is an example of an activity report with direct costs assigned to each activity such as bibliographic checking and book distribution. Unlike traditional budget reports that are separated into expenditure categories such as supplies, the activity report in figure 3.1 has two separate cost groupings.

FIGURE 3.1

Activity Report for Technical Services Department

DEPARTMENT: Technical Services

MISSION OBJECTIVE: To assist users in easily locating library materials

ACTIVITY COST REPORT
For the Month Ended March 31, 20xx

	MONTHLY ACTUAL
PART I: Department	
Bibliographic checking	$ 2,500
Payment card procurement	130
Book distribution	575
Original book cataloging	4,000
Original periodic cataloging	3,400
Re-cataloging books and periodicals	500
Withdrawing materials	375
Online catalog maintenance	525
Shelf list maintenance	600
Personnel services	6,975
Administrative duties	4,500
Training	880
Total cost of department activities	$24,960
PART II: Nondepartment traceable costs	
Technology**	3,000
Total department cost	$27,960

* Includes purchase price, startup cost, and a current cost of technology

The first cost section, department activity, lists the cost of the primary activities within the department, and although not shown, each of these activities can be further subdivided into tasks. For example, the tasks in withdrawing a book include locating and removing a book from the collection, pulling the card from the catalog or making the entries into online catalog, and updating all records to reflect the change in the collection. Naturally, variations in the activities of departments from library to library can be expected. For illustrative purposes, it is assumed that only books are being processed, but in another library with a multimedia processing environment, the activities should be redefined.

The second cost section of the activity cost report lists any nondepartment costs that are traceable to the department. From the overall library perspective, an objective of activity reporting is to trace unassigned overhead to specific departmental activities in the library. In this case, the traceable cost charged to technical services is a technology charge. The technology charge is for the services provided to Technical Services from the library's IT personnel and telephone charges traced directly to Technical Service employees. The IT staff loads updates to software used by Technical Services, installs new software, and keeps Technical Services computer systems running. Technical Services is therefore assigned a usage fee for these services that is part of the official budget allocation.

It is the department manager's responsibility to accept or reject how indirect costs are traced to his or her department. The acceptance of the method carries with it the responsibility for the costs. Initial acceptance must be mutually agreed upon within the organizational hierarchy and carefully considered to ensure that activities and decisions in another department are not driving up the costs of a second department to which these costs are traced. With the emphasis on activities, the interrelatedness of costs will be easier to identify and interdepartmental cost activities become easier to control.

Next, Sarah determines the percentage of administrative costs in her monthly expenditures. Administrative costs are equal to about 16 percent of total monthly expenditures. This percentage is not excessive, and therefore the department appears to have its administrative costs in balance relative to its total departmental costs as noted in Chapter 2. She has decided to focus her attention on bibliographic services and the technology charge allocated to the department.

Two professional library staff members perform bibliographic checking. Bibliographic checking consists of developing accurate bibliographic citations and holdings for library titles so books can be properly shelved and to prevent the library from unintentionally duplicating its titles. The activities in this area involve verifying bibliographic databases with library holdings and completing shelving labels for books that are added to the library's collection and databases.

The bibliographic staff processes books on a first-come, first-served basis. There currently is no standard for the number of citations that should be checked per hour by library assistants. Sarah has requested a breakdown from the accounting staff on technology charges and found that 30 percent of the department's technology charges are related to phone calls made to publishers and/or suppliers in checking orders or citations.

Sarah also reviewed charges on the payment cards. Payment card procurements are used for small purchases, and the charges have been running $130 for the month or approximately $1,560 annually. She decides to review these three items and training expenditures.

Sarah believes she can reduce the monthly cost of operations by taking the following actions:

Training costs will be cut by $400.

The operating procedures in bibliographic services will be changed. The creation of citations will no longer follow a first-come, first-served basis. Beginning immediately, a batch system will be adopted for identifying citations. The books will no longer be processed on a first-in, first-served basis. Instead, they will now be batched into groups related to the source where the citation is found. All batches will be processed when there are fifteen books in each grouping. This change may result in an increase in backlogged books, but it will free up the time of the librarians in bibliographic services.

The freed-up time in bibliographic services will be used to upload and update the library software used in Technical Services. Sarah will ask the director of the library to reduce the technology charge by $200 per month as Technical Services is taking over job functions from IT, and she does not feel the department should be charged for these activities.

The technology charge includes $900 in phone charges traceable to Technical Services. This charge is equal to approximately $6 per call. Sarah believes the making of 150 calls per month by the two librarians in Technical Services is unnecessary. These calls are being made to vendors and publishers regarding book citations. She has decided to limit the number of calls to 25 for each assistant for a savings of $600 (dropping 100 calls). Again, this may result in a higher backlog of books waiting for citations.

Pay card procurements are made for small purchases such as miscellaneous supplies and other small items. Sarah is worried that the director of the library will not reduce her technology charge. As part of her budget reduction plan, she has withdrawn the P-cards from Technical Services and required all miscellaneous payments on the P-cards to go through her office. She expects that with less books being purchased by the library, the miscellaneous payments will automatically be reduced, and this will provide the remainder of the cost reductions she needs to meet a 5 percent reduction in her budget. If this does not work, she is prepared to release one of her student workers.

Under traditional budget cutting, expenditure areas such as supplies, travel, and salaries would be reviewed and each item on the list would be required to return 5 percent of its budget allocation. Many mangers operate in this manner without analyzing their financial data to identify the activities that are driving costs up. Many of these activities can be cut without reducing the overall quality of services to the NP's patrons.

Sarah has made an attempt to review the bibliographic activities that are performed in Technical Services. She is attempting to change the way those activities that drive costs are performed in order to cut her budget. There are other activities that are performed in Technical Services such as cataloging, withdrawing of materials, and maintenance activities that would need to be reviewed during budget cutbacks. Still, this example is illustrative of the actions that could be taken by an NP department head at any NP.

When all these areas are under review, it is necessary to understand how cost drivers are expected to behave. Care must be exercised because as one activity is cut back, it may result in increasing other activities and their associated costs. Thus, it is important to understand the relationship between activities and costs. Without understanding how costs behave, incorrect assumptions may be made about how to reduce budget costs. It is also important to determine how overhead costs, such as the technology charges, become part of Technical Services budget. Such an understanding provides a way for department heads to reduce those charges or at least question the manner in which their department is charged. Such understandings are crucial to making the correct decisions when NPs are faced with budget reductions.

MORE COMPLEX ABM ANALYSIS

The Essex University Library is currently provided with a line-by-line budget report that classifies expenditures by departments according to expenditure types such as personnel salaries, travel, maintenance, supplies, and equipment. Expenditures for library services among two branches and the main library are all aggregated together in the budget report. The information in the report makes it impossible to identity costs by the activity that is causing the cost to increase. For example, the budget line "computer maintenance" includes computer services for Cataloging, Circulation, and Technical Services in this one item. It is impossible to determine how to reduce these costs when there is no information as to how they are incurred. The Director of the Library has determined that she will institute a pilot project in the Interlibrary Loan Department (ILL) to identify which activities are creating cost increases within the ILL.

The ILL is staffed with one professional librarian, Alice Ward, and two staff members who spend 90 percent of their time working on departmental activities. The librarian has indicated that 60 percent of her time is devoted to interlibrary loan activities and the other 40 percent of her time is devoted to activities such as reference committee assignments, meetings, other non-loan department activities such as special projects and training. Salaries for the department total $92,000. The librarian receives an annual salary of $45,000. Mailing costs in the department equal $35,000 per year and on-campus mailing costs are minimal. It is estimated that the mailing costs are divided between requested materials from Essex University Library's patrons and materials being requested by other ILLs at 70 and 30 percent, respectively. The department has collected the following information about its activities:

- Ten percent of the interlibrary loans are for materials that are already in the library's collection.
- Average number of ILL department requests sent to patrons in order to get circulated materials back into the ILL is as follows: faculty (5), undergraduates (1), and graduate students (2).
- Average number of requests needed to successfully receive materials is 1.2 requests from loaning libraries.
- Average number of interlibrary loans is 9,750 (books, 6,000; articles, 3,750).
- Average number of annual external requests for our library materials is 5,500 (books, 4,500; articles, 1,000).

The director has asked Alice, the head of the ILL, to outline the activities that are performed within the department related to both loaning materials to other libraries as well as borrowing materials per patron requests. Alice is unfamiliar with activity-based accounting methods, but she developed an outline (figure 3.2) about her department's activities.

NO WORRIES, MATE

Last Library Branch Closes Today

The Southeast Branch of Lincoln Library, which has been open to city residents for 27 years, will close today, the victim of city budget cuts.

The West Branch closed, perhaps permanently, on Wednesday.

The closures were announced less than 24 hours after aldermen approved a spending plan for the next fiscal year that doesn't include funding for the branch libraries.[4]

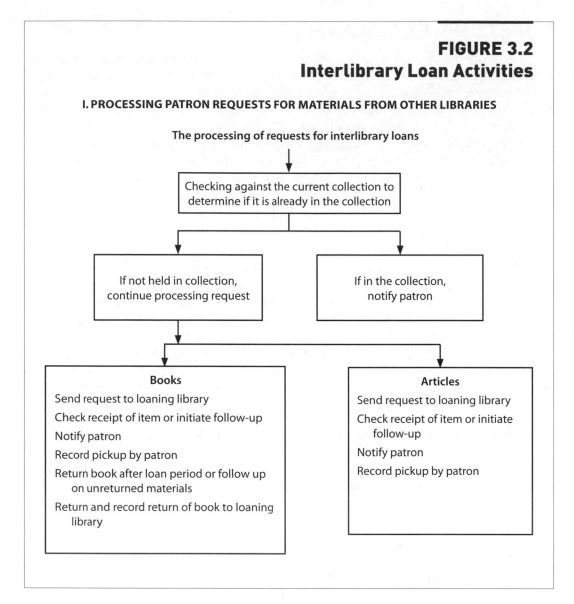

FIGURE 3.2
Interlibrary Loan Activities

I. PROCESSING PATRON REQUESTS FOR MATERIALS FROM OTHER LIBRARIES

The processing of requests for interlibrary loans

Checking against the current collection to determine if it is already in the collection

If not held in collection, continue processing request

If in the collection, notify patron

Books
Send request to loaning library
Check receipt of item or initiate follow-up
Notify patron
Record pickup by patron
Return book after loan period or follow up on unreturned materials
Return and record return of book to loaning library

Articles
Send request to loaning library
Check receipt of item or initiate follow-up
Notify patron
Record pickup by patron

The director and the head of Interlibrary Loans have been meeting for an hour and a half trying to determine how to assign costs to the various activities performed within the department. Can you help them find the unit cost of activities? The solution to this problem is in the appendix.

SUMMARY

Many NP managers are faced with crisis-level budget reductions. Historically, there have been decreases in NP funding, but afterward the funds always began to flow again. Today, the funding environment has changed, and no one can truly predict the length of the downturn in funding or when the next economic shock will occur. NP managers are faced with several choices: they can merge with other NPs, make severe cutbacks in their services, terminate their operations, or try to reduce costs in a logical manner.

The last alternative means the manager must have the financial skills to make informed financial decisions. The traditional financial reports prepared for NP managers do not

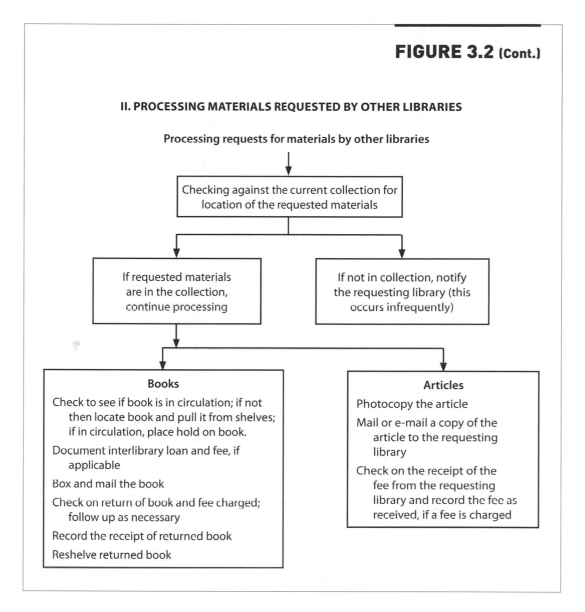

FIGURE 3.2 (Cont.)

II. PROCESSING MATERIALS REQUESTED BY OTHER LIBRARIES

Processing requests for materials by other libraries

Checking against the current collection for location of the requested materials

If requested materials are in the collection, continue processing

If not in collection, notify the requesting library (this occurs infrequently)

Books

- Check to see if book is in circulation; if not then locate book and pull it from shelves; if in circulation, place hold on book.
- Document interlibrary loan and fee, if applicable
- Box and mail the book
- Check on return of book and fee charged; follow up as necessary
- Record the receipt of returned book
- Reshelve returned book

Articles

- Photocopy the article
- Mail or e-mail a copy of the article to the requesting library
- Check on the receipt of the fee from the requesting library and record the fee as received, if a fee is charged

allow for informed decision making. By training themselves, managers must determine if it possible to salvage any of the information in these reports or whether it is necessary to develop their own financial analysis. The first three chapters have laid the groundwork for the development of financial skills. The next chapter will further develop skills needed to help an NP organization to survive a budget crisis.

NOTES

1. Jeff Rowe, "County Recommends 10 Percent Budget Cuts." *North Country Times,* February 3, 2009, www.nctimes.com/news/local/swcounty/article_21e46d8c-81d9-5af3-b067-b6bf1bb304ea.html.

2. Debbie Gilbert, "Budget Cuts Might Slice State Parks in Northeast Georgia," *Gainesville Times .Com,* August 29, 2008, www.gainesvilletimes.com/news/archive/8185/.

3. Norman Oder, "Phoenix Public Library Faces 21.4% Budget Cut; Six of 15 Branches Would Close," *Library Journal,* February 2, 2010, www.libraryjournal.com/article/CA6717294.html.

4. Deana Poole, "Last Library Branch Closes Today," *State Journal-Register,* February 4, 2010, www.sj-r.com/top-stories/x231973920/Last-library-branch-closes-today.

FOUR

COST BEHAVIOR: THE GOOD, THE BAD, AND THE UGLY

Behavior: The manner in which something functions or operates: the faulty behavior of a computer program; the behavior of dying stars.

Dictionary.com

Although it may appear that an NP manager's primary concern is simply not to overspend his budget, the costs of operations become critical as the NP finds its budget allocation and other funding disappearing. As funding sources are reduced, the primary question changes to how we can continue to provide services if we are continually underfunded. At that point, it is important to know how costs behave.

In the previous chapter, one issue facing Sarah and Alice as department head and director, respectively, was determining how costs behave with changes in activity levels. Or, with the case of Sarah, how costs are assigned to her department. Cost behavior patterns need to be considered as decisions are made to cut budgets or to buy new equipment, for example. Although most of the expenditures faced by NPs are fixed costs, such as staff salaries, not all expenditures are fixed as some change with the level of services provided to patrons. The percentage of total costs that change with the volume of services varies from one NP organization to another. For example, the variable costs at a food bank would make up of a larger portion of its budget than the variable costs found in a museum. This chapter describes several useful cost terms and ideas, and it provides examples of why cost analysis is important in NP decision making.

Costs are all the resources used by the NP to meet its mission objectives. Our costs are usually the price someone charges us for goods or services. Yet, costs must be correctly assigned to time periods to determine the expenses of periods such as in a month or year. Costs can be used to purchase an asset, such as a vehicle, or costs can be expended without creating any future benefit to the organization beyond the current period. Salary expenses are an example of a cost that only benefits the current period; whereas, asset purchases benefit more than one time period. Eventually, long-lived assets turn into an expense

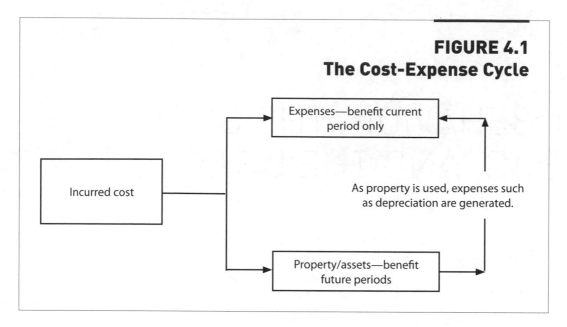

FIGURE 4.1
The Cost-Expense Cycle

over time as their usefulness disappears. The change is recorded in the accounting records as depreciation. Expenses and the change of long-lived cost into an expense are shown in figure 4.1.

WHAT DOES COST REALLY MEAN?
TELL ME . . . BRIEFLY!

Before the behavior of costs are considered, costs for managerial reporting need to be defined in more detail and separated from budgeted allocations.

Actual Costs

What are the actual costs involved in decision making? Actual costs are costs incurred at the time a transaction takes place. A service is provided to the NP or goods are purchased by the NP, and in return the NP organization either incurs a debt or makes a cash payment. Costs are not defined as a budget appropriation and they are not found in a budget report. Budget reports will not provide cost information as budget reports are based on legal spending limits, and those legal limits can be reset by policy makers. For example, the purchase of a copy machine creates a cost that may appear as equipment appropriation in a budget report, but the total cost of that machine is not part of the cost of running the department in the current period. Only a portion of the machine's cost contributes to running the department in the current period. For most managerial decisions, actual costs need to be "sliced and diced" to determine how much a service is really costing the NP. Without knowing the cost of operations or the future direction of cost trends, the budget will need continual increases every year. If an NP's budget can be increased yearly without any problems, then there is no need to be concerned about the cost of operations.

Budgeted "Costs"

There is no such cost as a budgeted cost. Budgeted amounts are related to legal spending limits of resources for a time period such as a year. Each NP uses an annual budget, but its costs of operation are not equal to those budgeted allocations, and there is little, if any, correlation between efficient operations and budgets. Budget dollars simply show what can be spent during a specific time period, and meeting budget guidelines only shows that spending was kept within defined limits. Budgeted dollars do not show your cost of operations. They simply convert the political allocation of resources into numbers.

Expired Costs (Expenses)

Expired or consumed costs are assigned to the proper time periods for financial reporting purposes and are called expenses. Expenses are the costs incurred that have no visible future benefit beyond the current time period.

Deferred Costs (Assets)

Costs that have not expired or have not been consumed are considered to be costs that are deferred to the future to be used in a future time period. Examples of deferred costs are equipment, vehicles, supplies, and buildings. Paper supplies are purchased from budget allocations in the current period, but unless they are all used in the current period a portion of these costs is deferred to the future. These deferred costs are called assets.

Allocated Costs: A Complication

For cost data to be useful for managerial decision-making purposes, costs must be dissected and assigned to service activities. In a library, service activities are found in Circulation and the Children's Library, for example. In a museum, service activities are found in a Museum School and Cultural History Exhibit. These departments have direct contact with the NP's patrons. The direct costs of each department, such as salaries, can be traced to that department. Yet there are many other administrative and support activities performed within the NP that cannot be traced to specific programs. Each of these activities has a cost.

These untraceable administrative costs are either implicitly or explicitly allocated to the program departments serving the public. An example of an explicitly allocated cost is the Technology charge that had been allocated to Technical Services as explained in the previous chapter. A portion of the Technology charge was for IT services provided to Technical Services. The IT charge itself could include the cost of depreciation on IT equipment as well as a portion of salaries and wages paid in the IT department. Again, allocating these amounts provides a means to find out the total cost of operations, which is different from the budget allocations. Allocation policies are used because service costs are difficult to trace directly to specific patron services provided by the library. Alice, who was head of Technical Services, has little control over the allocated IT charges that were passed on to her department. The cost was assumed to be allocated in a "reasonable" manner so that the full cost of her department could be determined.[1] Alice was trying to get this charge reduced.

> ## ALLOCATE THOSE COSTS AWAY!
>
> From a financial standpoint, we're able to do things at a lower cost than other nonprofits, so foundation support we receive goes further, more of it goes to journalism, less of it goes to overhead as a percentage. This is a clear distinction between ourselves and all the other nonprofits; the fixed costs with operating a news organization are distributed across the network. In 2008, we spent tens of thousands of dollars at the time on a redesign, but it was distributed across six sites.[2]

When allocated costs are implicitly passed on to the NP's service activities, they do not appear as a specific charge against each department such as the Technology charge. Instead of an explicit charge, these costs cause another department's budget to be reduced—there is only so much to go around. Most managers would not be aware that their budget is lower, so that department's budget for IT, for example, can be covered by the total budget allocation. When the charge is explicit as in Alice's case, she had to take action to have the charge reduced. If 10 percent budget reductions are instituted, one of the best areas to begin the cutting is with these implicit or explicit service costs.

Now that "costs" have been described, it is necessary to understand more about how costs behave. Some stay constant; some go up and make a right turn; and others just keep increasing.

IDENTIFYING THOSE SQUIGGLY COSTS

In the long run all costs have the ability to squiggle, but as time periods become shorter, some costs begin to wiggle less. In a twelve-month time period, some costs will not change regardless of the decisions made by managers. Some of these costs will remain stable even when departmental services are cut. So, does it do any good to cut services?

At this point a few different cost terms and their behavioral effects need to be considered. The costs that are described here will be the ones that NP managers need to most clearly understand so they can relate activities to the changes in how these costs behave.

Fixed, Variable, and Mixed Costs

Separating costs into fixed, variable, or mixed costs is important in analyzing cost behavior and in making managerial decisions. Cost-behavior patterns affect decisions about the savings or cost increases that are likely to occur from changes in activities or service levels. Remember that the time period under which these costs are being defined is one year. This arbitrary designation of a one-year time frame means that care should be exercised when separating fixed and variable costs in this manner. For example, a cost recognized as a fixed cost in a one-year time frame may be the most rapidly changing, or variable, cost in a two-year time frame.

A fixed cost is a cost that does not change as the level of services within a library changes. Rent and insurance are examples of fixed costs. The salaries of all contract employees are fixed and will not change directly with the library services provided. The law of averages can make your NP appear to be more efficient because of fixed costs. Simply dividing by more activities or units into total fixed costs reduces fixed cost on a per unit basis and makes our total per unit costs go down. Are we a better organization? Are we more efficient because total per unit costs decreased? No. We are not providing better services; we are just providing more services. So, if you are evaluated on a per unit basis, produce more activity.

If a cost changes as the volume of services changes, it is a variable cost. Some costs may vary, but they must vary directly with volume levels, not time, to be considered a variable cost. Supplies used in the technical services department are an example of a variable cost. Hourly wages paid to staff assistants are another example of variable costs because as service levels increase, so do hours worked by staff assistants and total wage costs.

Some costs, however, may be variable or fixed depending on how they are calculated. For example, depreciation on a bookmobile may be a fixed amount every year, or the expense could vary with the number of miles logged on the bookmobile. Depreciation expense may vary with time periods, but unless it varies directly with services—hours of use and

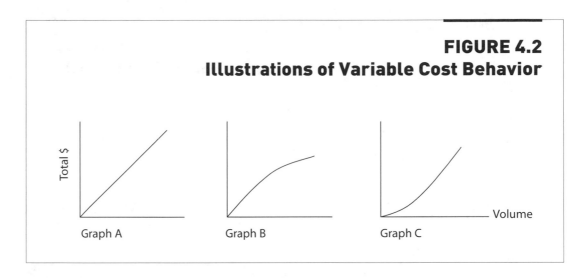

FIGURE 4.2
Illustrations of Variable Cost Behavior

Total $ (vertical axis) · Volume (horizontal axis)

Graph A   Graph B   Graph C

mileage—it is not a variable cost. The key is whether the cost changes as activities or service levels change, and, of course, the type of activity will vary with the NP and even the department under consideration.

Figure 4.2 provides three illustrations of variable costs. Graph A in figure 4.2 is the typical example of a variable cost—a 45-degree line between total variable cost and volume of services. Graphs B and C are also examples of variable costs, but they change at decreasing and increasing rates, respectively, with volume of service. Both graphs B and C are illustrations of variable costs because they vary with the volume level of services provided. If the horizontal axis were changed to a measure of time instead of a volume level, none of these costs would be considered a variable cost.

Although it may be useful to separate all costs into fixed and variable costs, this practice may ignore the way some costs behave. Some costs do not exhibit all the characteristics of either a fixed or variable cost. These costs can be called mixed costs because they have characteristics of both variable and fixed costs. An example of a mixed cost is found in the way total salaries for supervisors behave when the span of control is considered. One supervisor can efficiently handle a specific number of employees, but as employees are added beyond a certain number, other supervisory personnel must be added to help with the supervision tasks. The salary cost pattern

SO HOW DID YOU FIGURE THAT OUT?

Is This Correct?

Running school buildings and paying fixed costs would cost 5 percent more next year, while spending on everything else—books, salaries, busing, administration and more—would dip about 1 percent. Unnamed source. Comment: Oh, but salaries and administration are fixed costs, too.

Variable What?

Ten private pediatric practices in the Denver, Colorado, metropolitan area participated in the study. There were 37 different agreements between the health plans and practices for vaccine administration payments. The total documented variable cost per injection (excluding vaccine cost) averaged $11.51, calculated from the following categories: nursing time, $1.71; billing services, $2.67; non-routine services, $1.64; registry use, $0.96; physician time, $4.05; supplies, $0.36; medical waste disposal, $0.12. The researchers concluded, "This study shows that the variable costs of vaccine administration exceeded reimbursement from some insurers and health plans."[3]

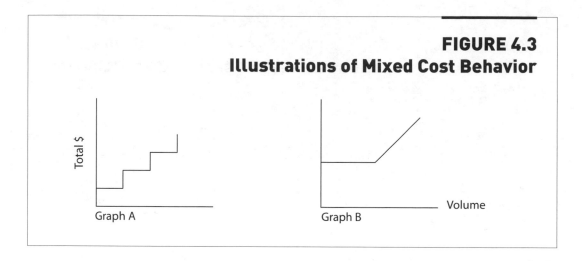

FIGURE 4.3
Illustrations of Mixed Cost Behavior

for total supervisors' salaries behaves as illustrated in figure 4.3, Graph A. As the end of an efficient span of control is reached, a new supervisor is added and total salary costs increase in a stair-step fashion. This mixed cost remains fixed for only a limited increase in the volume of service. Therefore, it is not fixed per se, but it does not show all the characteristics of a variable cost either.

Another example of mixed costs is illustrated in figure 4.3, Graph B. This cost pattern begins as a fixed cost and changes to a variable cost after a specific volume level is reached. Utility rates that begin with a flat charge and change to a variable rate per unit after a certain usage figure is reached are an example of this cost pattern.

These cost patterns show that it is important to understand cost patterns before assumptions about budget cuts can be made. In an NP facing budget cuts, knowledge of cost-behavior patterns aid the NP manager in initiating cost cuts with a minimum decline in value-added services. The decision involves more than simply curtailing activities or instituting across-the-board percentage budget cuts. For example, it may mean knowing the point of utility usage where rates start to increase steeply as a variable cost and avoid going over a specific level of utility usage. Some NPs have gone to four-day weeks to save budget dollars and one of their savings is related to utility usage.

DOES A 10-HOUR DAY
MEAN I GET OVERTIME?

Boynton Commission Weighs Workings of Winnowed Workweek

The four-day workweek, which began on June 8, has been a financial success, yielding $143,000 in savings, according to a report that will be presented to the city commission on Tuesday. The commission can then vote to continue the four-day workweek, modify it or return to the old five-day, eight-hour schedule.

Savings included lower electricity bills and air-conditioner use. Fuel consumption by public works employees dropped 28 percent.

For the library, Friday was a slow day anyway, reported director Craig Clark, who reported no customer complaints. "We have had conversations with customers (and) they were satisfied," Clark wrote.[4]

IS IT IMPORTANT TO OPERATE EFFICIENTLY? WHO KNEW?

There is nothing in an NP budget that determines whether an NP organization is providing services in an efficient manner. Meeting budget limits or not meeting them does not mean the organization is performing efficiently. All it means is that the NP did not overspend its budget. Should the NP return monies to its funding agency, it still does not mean the NP provided services to the public in an efficient manner. In some cases, the return of monies is done to curry favor from officials at the granting agency. There is a difference between providing efficient services and providing services under budget spending limits. Often, NPs or other government agencies have little concern about the relationship between the costs incurred and how efficiently services are provided.

If efficient operations are a concern, it begins with establishing standards for performance—for example, how many cases need to be processed by a caseworker or how many books should be shelved each hour. Efficiency is based on output levels compared to the input of resources into a service system. The behavior of actual costs compared to preset standard costs, not budget dollars, can be used to evaluate performance. When unit level standards are used, activity levels are incorporated into the evaluation. In the previous chapter, Alice, the Director of the Essex University Library was beginning to develop performance standards based on activities in the ILL.

Unlike allocated costs, standard costs can be useful in evaluating efficient performance. Standards can set predetermined activity levels that need to be reached by employees. Through past experience or the use of time and motion studies, it is possible to determine how long it should take to efficiently perform many routine activities. Activities such as shelf reading and book processing readily lend themselves to determining time/cost standards. The standards for time spent or materials used are established as cost performance criteria to be met by employees. The evaluation of efficient operations assesses whether the actual cost or processing rate is at least equal to a preset standard. With preset standards it is possible to evaluate service objectives to determine if they are being achieved efficiently. If actual costs do not meet the attainable standard, the differences need to be investigated so corrections can be made to reach efficient levels of operations.

An example of standard costs is the standard labor cost per book processed, which can be established based on attainable time and labor rates. These costs include the standard labor costs per hour for activities such as sorting, affixing labels, stamping and attaching pocket and date due slips, inserting Tattle Tape Strips, and sorting for distribution. The standard labor costs allow for determining if there is a dollar variance between the number of books actually processed and the number of books that should have been processed within the standard labor time allocated for the task. In other words, for the number of books processed, how many hours should have been used? This number should be compared to the actual number of hours used. The standard developed allows for including efficiency in work tasks.

It may appear the dollar variances between actual work performed and standards are similar to the differences between actual dollars expended and budget appropriations, but they are not. When standard costs are determined, efficiency is the primary consideration. With standards, an attempt is being made to determine if the staff is performing work at an efficient level. Such a comparison is used to evaluate management performance and service levels. None of this information is available in budget reports.

When the differences between budget appropriations and actual expenditures are determined, efficient work performance is not a concern. The difference between budget and actual expenditures is made to highlight deviations from board-approved spending levels only, which is a quasi-legal concern, not an efficiency consideration per se.

SOME OF MY FAVORITE COSTS

Before finishing a chapter on cost behavior, it is necessary to mention a few final cost ideas that are useful for NP managers. As managers go about trying to help their NP survive in an environment where it seems the future only holds further cuts in resources, these ideas are useful.

Who Did What to My Budget? Noncontrollable Costs

In the previous chapter, Sarah, head of Technical Services, was questioning why her budget allocations included a charge for IT services. At that point, she had made changes in the activities in Technical Services that would hopefully reduce a portion of this allocated charge. Such charges are called noncontrollable costs. In other words, they are charged against a department because of a policy decision, and they are not controllable by an NP manager.

As managers try to control their costs, it is important to separate controllable and noncontrollable costs. Without this cost separation, managers may be held accountable for costs over which they have no control or responsibility. A controllable cost is a cost that can be changed by a specific manager taking a specific action. An example of a controllable cost is the overtime incurred within a manager's department. In NP organizations, the costs themselves may not be controllable but the activities may be controllable; thus a shift in activities allows a noncontrollable cost to be reduced. Sarah was trying to accomplish this by changing activities within her department.

It also needs to be mentioned that a controllable cost will vary at different organizational levels within an NP. For example, the business manager may be directly responsible for the incurrence of maintenance costs, but to a department head in the NP organization, any maintenance costs allocated to her department are not controllable. As another example, consider the costs that are controllable by an NP board. One cost controllable by a board is the director's salary, but if a portion of that salary is allocated to departments within the NP in determining the full costs of its operations, those individual department heads will view that allocated cost as noncontrollable by them.

Only poor decision makers would hold an NP manager responsible for noncontrollable costs. Cost responsibility and cost controllability for a manager should coincide. Therefore, a manager's performance evaluation should include consideration of how well controllable costs are kept within standards. If a cost is noncontrollable, however, a manager's performance should not be evaluated based on its incurrence because those costs can be allocated in any manner.

When full costs, including allocated costs, are used in financial reports, controllable costs need to be separated from noncontrollable costs. In the previous chapter, the financial report for Technical Services clearly separated controllable costs from noncontrollable costs. Managers need to realize that they are responsible for those costs over which they exercise managerial control.

SUMMARY

This chapter provides a background to specific cost terms and ideas that become useful when an NP manager decides to try to control organizational operating costs. The chapter highlighted cost terms that are useful to managerial decision making. To make good managerial decisions about an NP's operations and service levels, managers must focus on decisions that affect the future. It is for that reason that these costs have been described in this chapter. The cost classifications described in this chapter are not found in budget reports. Budget reports classify all costs together on budget lines to ensure that appropriated budget dollars have not been exceeded. As a result, budget reports cannot be used for most managerial decision-making issues. Also, most budget reports do not provide for cost control except on a total expenditure basis. If the NP manager is only concerned with making sure the allocated budget does not exceed appropriations, then there is no need to study any management methods as management consists of simply checking two numbers against each other.

The cost classifications described here cannot be found on NP financial statements either. As constructed, financial statements do not provide cost information that is needed by operating managers for decision making. Therefore, NP managers need managerial reports based on cost information that allows them to make insightful decisions, and those will be reviewed in the next chapter.

NOTES

1. The main benefit from collecting this information is that full-cost comparisons can be made on a year-to-year basis within an NP, as well as with annual periods. Additionally, full-cost data may be required to receive reimbursements on work performed under grant agreements.

2. Laura McGann, "Center for Independent Media: Four Lessons from a Nonprofit That Raised $11.5 Million in Four Short Years," *Nieman Journalism Lab,* February 3, 2010, www.niemanlab .org/2010/02/center-for-independent-media-four-lessons-from-a-nonprofit-that-raised-11-5 -million-in-four-short-years/.

3. "Research from School of Public Health Has Provided New Information about Life Sciences," insurancenewsnet.com, February 4, 2010, http://insurancenewsnet.com/article.aspx?id=158271.

4. Lona O'Connor, "Boynton Commission Weighs Workings of Winnowed Work Week," Palm Beach Post News, January 31, 2010, www.palmbeachpost.com/news/boynton-commission-weighs -workings-of-winnowed-work-week-204742.html.

FIVE

LOOKING FOR VALUE . . . AND FINDING IT

Your true value depends on what you are compared with.

Bob Wells, editor for *Windows*
& .NET Magazine

It is time to deal with financial figures and tie them directly to value creation. Most NP managers work with annual budgets when they have to make financial decisions, and that is the initial approach taken here: a discussion of the annual budget. Afterwards, the budget will be changed into a format that allows for NP decision making based on patron value generation not just spending limits.

For an NP organization, the major goal of the annual budget process is to institute and monitor spending guidelines. Of course, budgeted spending may have to be reduced if it becomes apparent that anticipated funding will not be received. To ensure that expenditure plans do not exceed preapproved budget guidelines, actual spending levels have to be closely monitored throughout the year. This comparison is usually performed on a monthly basis.[1] The purpose of a monthly report is to show the funds remaining to be spent on each budget item.

The difference between monthly and year-end variances should be noted at this point. The yearly budget variance is the difference between the total appropriation approved by the board for each budget item and the actual expenses for that budget item. There are a number of ways to subdivide such an annual appropriation into monthly allocations. The simplest method is to divide the yearly budget amounts by twelve to arrive at monthly figures. This is called a static budget, and it serves to control spending during intervals throughout the year. This method is acceptable for budgetary appropriations that will remain fixed over the annual period such as supervisory salaries, for example. In this case it makes sense to simply divide budget appropriations by twelve as it tends to correspond with payroll periods. Depending on the nature of services provided by an NP organization, up to 80 percent of their budget appropriation may be fixed or legally mandated. For such organizations, the remainder of the chapter may provide interesting reading, but limited room for shifting funds to support patron-valued services.

At noted in Chapter 4, costs can also vary with the volume of services provided. For example, the cost of medications provided at a public health clinic will vary with the number of patients or the cost of food provided in a food bank program varies with the number of people using the food bank. Thus, depending on the nature of services provided by the NP, a more meaningful method for monthly allocations may be based on volume levels, the number of library users, for example.

TRADITIONAL BUDGET REPORTS: A LEGAL FOCUS

A number of choices must be made in determining how an annual budget report should be prepared. For example, expense data are usually aggregated by object of expense, activity, program, department, or some combination of these expense classifications. It is not necessary to choose just one of these methods because budget reports can be reformatted to the required needs of the NP manager. To be complete, budget reports should show the amount of funds that have been committed for purchases that have not yet been received. Such committed purchases are called encumbrances. These purchases are considered to be outstanding until they are received. Encumbrances need to be shown on budget reports together with the actual amount of funds spent in order to reflect the total level of funding legally committed (i.e., actual spending plus encumbrances).

The first two budget reports in the chapter are traditionally formatted budgets except that they include two variances: (1) a cost variance, based on the difference between allocated budget appropriations and actual expenses, and (2) an expended variance that includes the added effect of encumbrances. In the reports, the only difference between a cost variance and an expended variance is the outstanding encumbrances. In table 5.1, the first example of a traditional budget report is shown. These budget items are listed by object of expenditure which is the common practice. The first column lists the budget item for which expenditures are budgeted. Column two, "Budget Appropriation," lists the legal budget appropriation approved by the board or other legal body. Column three, "Incurred Expenses," is the total of expenses incurred by the library during the year. The cost variance, shown in column four, is the difference between the actual cost of operations and legally approved budget appropriation. Budget reports usually omit column four and only show a total expended variance but not a cost variance. If the NP director spends more than authorized, it is recorded as an unfavorable variance in column seven. There are a number of unfavorable variances shown in table 5.1.

The second variance in table 5.1 is found in column seven, and it is the variance shown on most traditional budget reports. In calculating this variance, any outstanding encumbrances at the end of the year, column five, are added to the incurred expenses, column three. This total is placed on column six as the "Total Expended." The difference between the amounts in column six and column two is called the "Total Expended Variance" in column seven. This variance shows the difference between the board-approved budget funding and the actual expenses and encumbrances (i.e., outstanding orders). The director of the NP is not authorized to spend more than is allowed in the budget.

Both variances provide different information for the manager. The cost variance is the difference between the legally approved budget appropriation and actual expenses incurred during the year. The expended variance shows the effect outstanding encumbrances have on the cost variance. Both variances have a place in managerial decision making. The cost variance provides information about the actual cost of operations that is not available from the expended variance. The expended variance shows whether board-approved spending limits were followed. For example, a department head may attempt to encumber monies at the end of the year and overspend the budget with the hope that the encumbered amounts

TABLE 5.1

Annual budget report using line-item reporting based on objects of expenditure

Traditional Budget Report—Budget and Actual for the Year Ended June 30, 20xx

BUDGET ITEM [1]	BUDGET APPROPRIATION [2]	INCURRED EXPENSES [3]	COST VARIANCE* [4]	TOTAL OUTSTANDING ENCUMBRANCES [5]	TOTAL EXPENDED [6]	TOTAL EXPENDED VARIANCE* [7]	BUDGET PERCENT EXPENDED (%) [8]
Salaries	$130,000	$125,000	$5,000	$ —	$125,000	$ 5,000	96
Wages	26,000	30,000	(4,000)	—	30,000	(4,000)	115
FICA	10,000	10,250	(250)	—	10,250	(250)	103
Health	7,500	7,250	250	—	7,250	250	96
Retirement	14,000	13,500	500	—	13,500	500	96
Insurance	2,000	2,000	—	—	2,000	—	100
Building maintenance	6,500	6,000	500	750	6,750	(250)	104
Janitorial supplies	1,000	1,100	(100)	250	1,350	(350)	135
Utilities	9,000	11,000	(2,000)	—	11,000	(2,000)	122
Telephone	3,000	2,900	100	—	2,900	100	96
Postage	1,300	1,450	(150)	—	1,450	(150)	112
Photocopying	3,300	3,500	(200)	—	3,500	(200)	106
Audit fees	2,500	3,500	(1,000)	—	3,500	(1,000)	140
Petty cash expenses	300	300	—	—	300	—	100
Books	39,000	39,000	—	2,500	41,500	(2,500)	106
Periodicals	3,000	3,000	—	1,000	4,000	(1,000)	133
Equipment maintenance	2,000	1,500	500	—	1,500	500	75
Library supplies	4,000	3,800	200	500	4,300	(300)	108
Office supplies	2,100	1,900	200	500	2,400	(300)	114
Binding	700	750	(50)	—	750	(50)	107
Auto maintenance	500	600	(100)	750	1,350	(850)	270
Auto operations	800	700	100	—	700	100	88
Travel	500	—	500	—	—	500	0
Publicity	350	400	(50)	—	400	(50)	114
Totals	$269,350	$269,400	$ (50)	$ (6,250)	$275,650	$(6,300)	

*Unfavorable amounts in parentheses

will be paid for in the new budget year. When the expended variances are reported, such a tactic becomes readily apparent as an unfavorable variance.

Column eight shows the percent of the budget appropriation expended during the year. The percent is determined by dividing column two into column six. If the percent in column eight is more than 100 percent, it shows that more was spent and encumbered than had been appropriated for budget spending. In table 5.1, it can quickly be seen that auto maintenance was overspent by 270 percent.

This traditional budget report prepared at the end of the year is useful for identifying variances by objects of expenditure, such as salaries, wages, and so forth. The manager needs to determine the value added to NP patrons' services by these budget items. Quickly, it becomes apparent that such a determination is impossible. Also, with a year-end budget report, it is too late to take corrective actions to reduce excessive spending levels that have already occurred. Again, the need for at least monthly reports is emphasized.

In reviewing table 5.1, there are some conclusions that can be reached about spending levels. Unfavorable or favorable spending levels are identified through the budget variances shown in the report. Variances selected for investigation should include both significant favorable and unfavorable variances. It may be important to know the reason spending on a budget item fell below its appropriation. For example, in table 5.1, the reason there is a favorable variance of $5,000 in salaries should be investigated. A favorable variance may signal misallocated appropriations whereby excessive funds are provided in one area while underfunding a second area.

Review of the budget items in table 5.1 shows that the incurred expenses for building maintenance did not exceed the budget appropriation until the outstanding encumbrances are taken into account. When the outstanding encumbrances are included, a favorable variance of $500 is changed into an unfavorable variance of $250. This trend is apparent in the total of the expended variance column, and this overspending may be a tactic used to try to over-spend budget allocations. The total cost variance is unfavorable by $50 (column four), but when outstanding encumbrances are considered, it is unfavorable by $6,300 (column seven).

Problems can arise when a budget report such as the one shown in table 5.1 is used to analyze variances. This budget report only shows line items for the entire library, making it difficult to determine which department in the library is responsible for overspending. For example, the unfavorable wage variance of $4,000 in column four cannot be traced to departments. Also such a report provides little indication about how value is created for patrons. It is impossible to identify value creating activities from those activities that create no value. Traditional budget reports, such as in table 5.1, can be considered to be reports developed for the accounting staff by the accounting staff, but not for use in NP managerial decision making.

When the manager of an NP organization is faced with a crisis in funding and is required to use a budget report as shown in table 5.2, there is little that manager can do other than make across-the-board budget cuts or call for the elimination of funding in specific budget lines—for example, cut salaries by 12 percent. Such a budget report does not allow for managers to identify areas that add little or no value to patron services (non-value activi-ties) and make cuts there.

Table 5.2 shows an example of a budget report for a small library that isolates budget vari-ances by departments such as the Children's Library, Technical Services, and Maintenance. Budget data are presented in an object-of-expenditure format by department. Although the information in table 5.2 is summarized for three departments, all the library departments should be shown using a similar budget report.

As the budget report in table 5.1 is compared with the report in table 5.2, several differ-ences are noted. One difference is the ease with which it is possible to determine specific

TABLE 5.2

Budget report based on line items and departmental divisions

Traditional Budget Report—Budget and Actual for the Year Ended June 30, 20xx

BUDGET ITEM [1]	BUDGET APPROPRIATION [2]	INCURRED EXPENSES [3]	COST VARIANCE* [4]	TOTAL OUTSTANDING ENCUMBRANCES [5]	TOTAL EXPENDED [6]	TOTAL EXPENDED VARIANCE* [7]	BUDGET PERCENT EXPENDED (%) [8]
Children's Library							
Wages	$13,000	$12,500	$500	—	$12,500	$500	96
FICA	1,500	1,475	25	—	1,475	25	98
Books	4,000	3,900	100	$ 300	4,200	200	105
Periodicals	800	790	10	—	790	10	98
Library supplies	120	150	(30)	100	250	(130)	208
Office supplies	75	60	15	—	60	15	80
Totals	$19,495	$18,875	$620	$(400)	$19,275	$220	
Technical Services							
Salaries	$20,000	$20,000	—	—	$20,000	—	100
Wages	14,000	13,500	$500	—	13,500	500	96
FICA	3,000	2,950	50	—	2,950	50	98
Health	975	970	5	—	970	5	99
Retirement	1,200	1,175	25	—	1,175	25	98
Equip. maintenance	170	200	(30)	—	200	(30)	118
Library supplies	2,000	2,400	(400)	—	2,400	(400)	120
Office supplies	300	270	30	$ 30	300	0	100
Binding	300	350	(50)	—	350	(50)	117
Totals	$41,945	$41,815	$ 130	$(30)	$41,845	$100	
Maintenance							
Wages	$10,000	$15,000	$(5,000)	—	$15,000	$(5,000)	150
FICA	1,000	1,100	(100)	—	1,100	(100)	110
Janitorial supplies	1,000	1,100	(100)	$ 250	1,350	(350)	135
Build. maintenance	6,500	6,000	500	750	6,750	(250)	104
Totals	$18,500	$23,200	$(4,700)	$(1,000)	$24,200	$(5,700)	

*Unfavorable amounts in parentheses

responsibility for budget variances. For example, table 5.1 shows a $4,000 unfavorable variance in wages in the budget report, but without more investigation, it is impossible to determine which departments were responsible for the unfavorable variance. In the budget report in table 5.2, however, it is plain to see that the unfavorable variances of $5,000 in Maintenance and the favorable wage variance of $500 in both the Children's Library and the Technical Services Department were responsible for the overall unfavorable variance of $4,000. By locating the reason for the variance, it is possible to focus attention on the unfavorable variance in Maintenance and ignore the other two favorable as they are insignificant.

This budget report assigns departmental responsibility for variances. Once this determination is made, and if the variances are considered significant, they can be analyzed in more detail to determine their causes. Many of the variances in the budget report simply show the change in a fixed cost. For example, a new employee being hired could result in actual expenditures being more than budgeted appropriations which is recorded as an unfavorable variance. Yet, a wage variance also may be due to change in the number of hours worked. Within such variable cost variances, more detailed information as to the reasons for the variance needs to be identified. For example, the unfavorable wage variance could occur because higher wages had to be paid—a salary spending variance—or because excessive labor hours were used on a library activity—a work efficiency variance.[2] Because the cause of a variance affects the prescription for correcting that variance, causes must be determined as accurately as possible. When expenditures are classified according to departments, an NP manager can identify a department that may not be pulling its weight in meeting the NP's mission, and concentrate budget cuts within that department.[3] Still, the manager cannot cut specific non-value activities because they are not identified in table 5.2. Consequently, budget cuts would be targeted in those departments where it is assumed cuts can be made without significantly reducing patron services. When a traditional budget is used, crisis cuts tend to occur in facilities maintenance causing deterioration and years of deferred maintenance to accumulate.

FINDING VALUED ACTIVITIES

In using activity analysis, managerial efforts are devoted to reducing the costs of non-value activities—those activities that do not contribute to increasing patron services. To use this approach, activities must be divided into those that contribute to meeting patron service objectives (value-added activities) and those that do not (non-value-added activities).

The primary patron service objectives of a specific NP organization will vary. Therefore, differences exist in the definition of value-added activities from one organization to another. If an activity does not directly contribute to the achievement of a patron-service objective,

CAN'T FIND VALUE THERE? . . . FIRE THE POLICE

Sutter Creek is projecting a $80,568 deficit at the end of the current fiscal year June 30.

"You just can't afford to have a fully staffed police department," said Crosby, who suggested Sutter Creek turn over patrol duties to the Amador County Sheriff's Office. "I think we should get our police lined up the way Pine Grove does theirs," he said.

When it was pointed out that Pine Grove doesn't have a police department, Crosby smiled and replied, "I know."[4]

it is considered to be a non-value-added activity. Examples of non-value-added activities are reporting, moving materials, sorting, storing, counting, recording, or checking. The time devoted to these activities generates non-value-added costs. They reduce the service level to the patrons of the library because resources that should be devoted to patron services are misallocated. Other examples of non-value-added activities are the time spent for departmental parties, jury duty, docked time not reported, activities involving promotion or the tenure process, shutting offices at lunch time when patrons have time to come to university offices, university-wide committee meetings, continuous recruiting, compiling workload statistical summaries, compiling reports that have no actual purpose, administrative personnel performing tasks that should be assigned to lower-level personnel, preparing budgets or strategic plans that are later rejected, many staff and administrative services, and wasted idle time during holiday periods when NP's see a decrease in patrons. A number of activities performed within an NP add no value to the patron-oriented objectives. The time devoted to these activities (as well as their associated costs) need to be reduced first when an NP is facing a budget crisis. Many times these activities and their costs are part of the organization's general overhead and thus they are hard to identify and eliminate. With no means to identify non-value-added activities, the traditional call arises for across-the-board 10 percent budget cuts with the resulting damage to customer service and the organization's mission.

A first step in determining whether a departmental activity is adding value is to relate it to the department's mission. Assume the primary mission for the Circulation Department is "to maximize the availability of library materials to patrons." Once a department's primary mission is outlined, all the activities and tasks of the department should be written down, as is illustrated in figure 5.1. This list of activities is an illustrative example of the activities that could occur in a library's Circulation Department. The exact type of activities performed, however, would vary among libraries.

After the mission objective is described and all the activities and tasks outlined, the cost related to these activities should be determined. In figure 5.1, the activities related to copy maintenance costs (adding paper and toner; issuing and charging mag cards with cash; making service calls; new machine selection) should be easily identified with the associated copy machine volume. Normally, all such costs would be classified under a Supplies heading in a traditional budget as illustrated in tables 5.1 and 5.2.

Another Circulation Department activity grouping in figure 5.1 is Fines and Billings. The costs related to Fines and Billings are largely fixed costs. For example, salary costs. Such costs are going to have to be allocated based on such factors as time logs related to billing and fines activity. The relationship between the cost driver (i.e., the activity that makes cost increase) and the cost will not be as direct as with copy maintenance costs. In carrying out this process, the cost drivers for each activity group in figure 5.1, part 1, will need to be identified.

Once the Circulation Department's costs are allocated to the department's cost drivers, it is possible to develop a budget report based on activities rather than by objects of expenditure. When table 5.3 is reviewed, the budget costs are classified by activities that occur within

FINDING VALUE

Dozens of city administrators started the weekend in meeting rooms with taxpayers, charting exactly what their agencies do and why. And then they asked their audiences which parts of those jobs taxpayers really want them to do.

That tell-and-ask format is the core of a series of workshops Mayor John Peyton is overseeing as a way to start talking with ordinary people about some ugly budget choices coming up.

Expecting somewhere between a $40 million and $60 million shortfall in the coming year's budget, Peyton is asking people to pick what parts of government are really important to them.[5]

FIGURE 5.1
Circulation Department Activities List

ACTIVITY	TASKS
1. Copy Machine Maintenance	Adding paper and toner Issuing and charging patron mag cards Making service calls New machine selection
2. Search-Holds	Handling search requests Reordering missing books and periodicals Recalling books
3. Circulation	Charging out books and periodicals Issuing library cards Answering questions Discharging books Recording the return of discharged materials Shelving in the stacks Checking for holds on returned materials
4. Fines and Billings	Collecting cash Processing overdue receipts and notices Processing receipts and notices for damaged and lost books and periodicals Filing receipts and notices
5. Exit Control	Processing magnetic protection strips for checkout Signing out interlibrary loans on clipboard
6. Stack Maintenance	Shelving items used and left unshelved Processing new books and shelving them Shelf reading books Shifting materials on stacks
7. Exhibit Preparation	Putting up and removing exhibits on bulletin boards, display cases, etc. Ensuring security of exhibits Handling exhibit promotion
8. Personnel Services	Dealing with the appointment, tenure, promotion, and retainment of personnel Interviewing new candidates Serving on search committees Preparing required evaluation forms for personnel files
9. Administrative Duties	Attending and conducting departmental meetings Preparing memos, workload statistics, board requested information Attending committee meetings Planning Preparing work schedules Ordering and receiving supplies
10. Training	On-site reading, writing, and studying training materials Attending workshops and conferences Visiting other libraries to study new methods and techniques

the Circulation Department. The monthly budget variances are shown by each identified activity. When an NP manager uses a budget formatted on activities rather than cost object (salaries, etc.), it becomes easier to identify areas for cost reduction rather than cutting every budget line by ten percent. For example, one of the activities under Administration in figure 5.1 is related to planning, work scheduling, ordering, and receiving supplies. The question needs to be raised as to whether it is possible to reduce these activities and their associated costs. Could software be purchased to automate these tasks? Can ordering and receiving of supplies be outsourced? If so, can some remaining Administrative costs be reassigned? The point is that as the budget is reformatted new questions related to budget reductions begin to be addressed from a different perspective. It should be noticed that the Circulation Department also receives a charge for IT services as a technology charge. This allocated budget item can only be reduced by a policy change by the director of the library.

Although the budget in table 5.3 provides useful information for the NP manager that cannot be found in a traditional budget, this information can still be reformatted to allow the manager to make even better decisions when it becomes necessary to reduce the budget. In

TABLE 5.3
Activity cost report for circulation

DEPARTMENT: Circulation

MISSION OBJECTIVE: To maximize the availability of library materials to patrons

ACTIVITY COST REPORT
For the Month Ended March 31, 20xx

	MONTHLY ESTIMATE	MONTHLY ACTUAL	VARIANCE *
PART I: Department			
Copy machine maintenance	$ 600	$ 500	$100
Search holds	400	425	(25)
Circulation	4,000	3,700	300
Fines and billings	315	300	15
Exit control	85	68	17
Stack maintenance	1,150	1,100	50
Exhibit preparation	115	125	(10)
Personnel services	5,600	5,625	(25)
Administrative duties	2,100	1,900	200
Training	475	400	75
Total cost of department activities	$14,840	$14,143	$697
PART II: Nondepartment traceable costs			
Technology**	3,700	3,700	0
Total department cost	$18,540	$17,843	$697

* Unfavorable amounts in parentheses

** Includes purchase price, startup cost, and a current cost adjustment fee for technology support costs order to take this next step, activities should be separated into those that do and those that do not assist in meeting the primary mission objective. For example, dealing with promotion and tenure tasks under Personnel Services in figure 5.1 does not directly contribute to the availability of library resources to patrons. Yet, in a university library, a great deal of time each year is devoted to promotion and tenure activities. Under Search-Holds, one of the activities is "recording missing books." Such an activity should be considered non-value-added because it is redundant. The library should be secure enough so that such an activity should not have a separate listing. . . . it should be insignificant. Therefore, it is a non-valued activity. The tasks associated with fine collections and billings do not have a direct impact on maximizing the availability of library materials to patrons under circulation's mission objective. If this activity could be transferred to the job functions of a central university cashier or computerized, it would reduce costs and increase the time available for Circulation Department personnel to achieve their primary objective. Efforts should be made to reduce activities and associated costs listed under the non-value-added column when cost curtailment becomes necessary. Once these non-value activities are reduced, it may become clear how much overstaffing exists in the library.

Once the value-added and non-value-added activities are separated, the costs associated with each activity need to be shown. Table 5.4 presents an activity cost report for the Circulation Department using the concepts of value-added and non-value-added activities and costs. The benefit of separating non-value-added costs from value-added costs is immediately obvious. The separation of these costs allows the NP manager to concentrate on reducing non-value-added activities and their costs. This focus allows for a more surgical approach to cost cutting rather than the use of across-the-board budget cuts which have to be used in conjunction with a traditional budget report.

When a budget report is organized around activities rather than object of expenditure reporting, identification of the specific non-valued activities and costs are easier to identify. Under activity analysis, cost cutting can be achieved by reducing non-value-added activities and keeping value-added activities and patron services largely intact. In reviewing table 5.4, it can be seen that exit control consists of $85 of non-value-added activities. Exit control activities need to be analyzed to determine if they can be automated. Personnel services, which make up about 38 percent of the budget appropriation, need to be reviewed to determine if the non-value activities and their costs ($5,000) can be reduced or at least reassigned to more value-added activities.

The reports in table 5.3 and table 5.4 can be compared as both reports are based on the same budget appropriation. Although both illustrations use an activity-based accounting approach, the reporting improvement shown in table 5.4 gives the department manager a place to take immediate action in curtailing costs by reducing non-value-added activities within each activity line on the budget. Such a cut would save Circulation $7,815 or close to 52 percent of its budget. Another way of viewing this information is that Circulation is currently spending 52 percent of its budget on non-value-added activities. The decision making based on these two budgets is different than when the budgets in tables 5.1 or 5.2 are used. The latter two budget reports allow little room for analysis of activities usually resulting in the traditional across-the-board cuts.

Finally, the identified variances in table 5.4 are not as important as knowing whether an activity added value. For example, there is a favorable variance with exhibit preparation, but the activity does not contribute value-added services to patrons; therefore, even with a favorable variance, the costs incurred by these activities should be eliminated.

A budget report using value- and non-value-added classifications is illustrated for a library in table 5.5. These activities and costs are separated into service and program departments. Service departments provide support services to each program. For example, the business

TABLE 5.4
Value-added and non-value-added activity cost report for the Circulation Department

DEPARTMENT: Circulation

MISSION OBJECTIVE: To maximize the availability of library materials to patrons

ACTIVITY COST REPORT
For the Month Ended March 31, 20xx

ACTIVITY	COST CLASSIFICATIONS				
	VALUE-ADDED ACTIVITY	NON-VALUE-ADDED ACTIVITY	MONTHLY ESTIMATED ACTIVITY	MONTHLY ACTUAL ACTIVITY	VARIANCE*
Copy machine maintenance	$ 200	$ 400	$ 600	$ 500	$100
Search holds	400	—	400	425	(25)
Circulation	4,000	—	7,000	6,200	800
Fines and billings	—	315	315	300	15
Exit control	—	85	85	68	17
Stack maintenance	150	1,000	1,150	1,100	50
Exhibit preparation	—	115	115	125	(10)
Personnel services	600	5,000	5,600	5,625	(25)
Administrative duties	1,400	700	2,100	1,900	200
Training	375	100	475	400	75
Total	$7,025	$7,815	$14,840	$14,143	$697

*Unfavorable amounts in parentheses

office provides accounting services to all programs. Program departments are those departments that provide services directly to patrons. The costs in table 5.5 are not classified by objects of expenditure such as supplies and wages, for example. Instead, department activities are first analyzed; then the costs of these activities are aggregated and reported as value-added and non-value-added cost groupings for the library. Supplemental schedules for each service department and program department should identify the non-valued and value-added activities in each area. It can be seen that 34 percent ($46,265/[$88,650 + $46,265]) of the budget expenditures are related to non-value-added activities.[6]

In the report, the variances are shown for each department, and the total monthly cost for which a manager is responsible is divided into value-added and non-value-added cost groupings. The method for allocating these traceable costs has been agreed upon by department

TABLE 5.5

Value-added and non-value-added activity cost report for the library director

DEPARTMENT: Library Director

MISSION OBJECTIVE: To maximize mission objectives of all departments

ACTIVITY COST REPORT
For the Month Ended March 31, 20xx

DEPARTMENT	EST. VALUE-ADDED ACTIVITY	EST. NON-VALUE-ADDED ACTIVITY	COST CLASSIFICATIONS			
			NONTRACEABLE	MONTHLY ESTIMATED DEPT. COST	MONTHLY ACTUAL DEPT. COST	VARIANCE*
Service departments						
Technical services	$21,250	$11,900	$ 3,200	$ 36,350	$ 35,800	$ 550
Public relations	7,750	1,350	1,700	10,800	11,000	(200)
Personnel	11,000	1,000	1,700	13,700	14,200	(500)
Business office	19,700	4,000	4,000	27,700	26,600	1,100
Program departments						
Circulation	7,025	7,815	—	14,840	14,143	697
Children's library	4,475	3,700	1,700	9,875	10,000	(125)
Special collections	3,200	2,800	1,500	7,500	7,300	200
Extension services	6,250	5,750	3,000	15,000	15,250	(250)
Reference	8,000	7,950	2,000	17,950	15,750	2,200
Total costs	$88,650	$46,265	$18,800	$153,715	$150,043	$3,672

*Unfavorable amounts in parentheses

heads, and they have accepted responsibility for the incurrence of these costs. Nontraceable costs, for which managers are not responsible, are the library's general overhead, which cannot be directly traced to a department. Such costs are usually assigned to program departments using a "reasonable" allocation method. These costs are listed separately in the report and include charges for technology and accounting services.

If a library director requires more detailed information about a department, the department's activity cost report may be reviewed. In such a case, a report like the one shown in table 5.4 for Circulation is available for each department. Unlike the traditional budget report, an activity budget report allows the manager to focus on those areas that are considered to be non-value-added activities. Now the NP manager can make selected cuts in the annual budget when the organization is dealing while maintaining patron services.

ACTIVITY-BASED MANAGEMENT

In a review of table 5.5, one question that arises is: Why is there a higher level of non-value-added costs in the program departments in comparison to the service departments (49 percent compared with 23 percent)?[7] A number of reasons could exist for this difference. First, the mission objectives of the five program departments may not be correctly stated. If the true mission objective is not properly described, activities that should be considered value-added are classified as non-value-added. Perhaps program departments are required to perform a number of activities that are not directly related to their primary function of serving patrons. As a result, they are only able to devote 51 percent of their activity and corresponding costs to value-added work that fulfills their mission. This difference in the levels of non-value-added activities in the program and service departments becomes readily apparent in an activity cost report. In traditional budget report, this difference is impossible to detect. Of course, once these activities are classified in this manner, it becomes management's responsibility to review the correspondence between mission objectives and activities.

Unlike traditional budgeting, budgeting based on activity analysis is more concerned with the effects of curtailed activities. For example, cutbacks in maintenance expenditures and activities over time will leave crippled equipment and a deteriorated physical facility. Such effects usually go unrecognized under traditional budgets. These cutbacks are easy to make in maintenance expenditures when a large percentage cut in overall budget appropriation is required. Under activity analysis, there is a higher possibility that these curtailed activities will be quickly detected because the activities occurring in the Maintenance Department are individually analyzed.

Once activity analysis is adopted, it allows departments to review departmental activities for inefficiencies. For example, questions such as these can be asked: Can a new system be adopted that would curtail non-value-added activity costs? Can branches be networked together for better integration of value-added activities? Upper-level managers can then review department activities to determine if duplicated activities can be eliminated or dovetailed with other activities and tasks. Afterwards, the question that needs to be asked is whether value-added activities are being efficiently performed.

NO VALUE THERE

"If we can't get savings in salaries, we have to look at pre-K, sports, arts and music," Johnson said. "We don't know to what extent."[8]

The next chapter will deal with evaluating performance measures in NP organizations from the perspective of activity analysis.

SUMMARY

The approach taken in the chapter has been to take a traditional budget and compare it with an activity-based budget without breaking from a traditional organizational structure. As explained in Chapter 1, it would be possible to change the NP's organizational structure to more closely follow value creation activities. Here that step was not taken. Instead, the approach showed how to use an activity-based budget within a traditional organization.

One advantage of activity analysis is that it is closely related to activity measures that many NPs already use to evaluate performance. Activity analysis takes the process one step further by relating accounting costs to the activity measures. In this way, activity analysis makes accounting data more interpretable. Under activity-based accounting, when cost reductions are necessary, they are made from the viewpoint of reducing the activities that create the costs. This cost-reduction program begins by reducing the cost of those activities generating non-value-added activities.

Even if an NP manager cannot get their hands on activity reports that are shown in the chapter, they can still begin to think of their operations as a conglomeration of activities. Consequently, instead of simply instituting across-the-board cuts, they can begin to try to identify those activities that do not contribute to the mission objectives.

It may seem that specific cutting of activities only cannot be done. NP organizations have done this for years. When the public refuses to pass a new tax increase—say, a city sales tax or a property tax—the city may take selective decreases in the budget to make it obvious to taxpayers that budget monies are needed. For example, the city may stop maintaining parks or cleaning the buildings and sidewalks. These are all selective budget cuts. If these cuts can be made in this fashion, then it is possible to make cuts to non-value-added activities and their associated costs. It can be done.

NOTES

1. With financial software, it is possible to have budget reports on a real-time basis and make daily comparisons.

2. Such a determination assumes that standard time for performing a task has been established.

3. Mission objectives are the long-range strategic objectives for a library, and although public service is the primary objective, slightly different objectives are found in different libraries: research, university, public, corporate, legal, and so forth. The mission objectives of a library help define departmental value-added and non-value-added costs and should be clearly outlined for each library and department before an activity-based accounting system is put into place.

4. Matthew Hedger, "Sutter Creek Tries to Balance Budget, City Councilman Thinks Police Should Go," *Ledger Dispatch*, March 5, 2010, www.ledger-dispatch.com/news/newsview.asp?c=266755&topStory=1.

5. Steve Patterson, "Budget Workshop Puts Jacksonville Taxpayers on Spot," March 7, 2010, http://jacksonville.com/news/metro/2010-03-07/story/budget_workshop_puts_jacksonville_taxpayers_on_spot.

6. The calculation excludes the nontraceable costs.

7. Forty-nine percent for the program departments is determined by adding all Program Department costs (both value-added and non-value-added) and then that total ($56,965) is divided into the total for non-value-added costs ($28,015). The same procedure is followed to determine the percentage for the Service Departments. Nontraceable costs are not used in determining these percentages.

8. Marcela Rojas, "Peekskill Schools Face 71 Staff Cuts, Ending Pre-K," www.lohud.com, March 7, 2010, www.lohud.com/article/20100307/NEWS/303070014/Peekskill-schools-face-71-staff-cuts-ending-pre-K.

SIX

PERFORMANCE: AN AFTERTHOUGHT?

It doesn't matter how valid your excuses, they will never change your performance.

Unknown

Activity analysis is recommended because it fits well into the traditional performance measurement systems of NP organizations. Instead of running a parallel system for accounting data and activities evaluation, the goals for an NP can be combined into one system. This merger creates a system with a strong commonsense orientation for those who are familiar with activity measures but not with accounting. In addition to this feature, activity analysis works well to help achieve the organizational mission objectives.

Once the value-added activities in an NP organization are identified, the manager should begin to question how effectively these activities are being performed. An NP organization wants to identify its value-added activities and then ascertain which of these activities are performed as effectively as possible. If patron services are delivered with lackadaisical attitudes and through the waste of scarce resources, managerial reports need to identify these problems. The current chapter and the next one are used to evaluate the performance of NP employees and managers. If the NP organization has a unionized work-force, it is unlikely such an organization could make the changes that are being suggested in this chapter. Also, these changes cannot be made in a hurry when the organization is being faced with closure. The described methods are changes that can be made in a viable organization to allow it to operate more efficiently and effectively.

STANDARDS FOR PERFORMANCE

Many NPs have established means for employee performance evaluation. Such evaluations of employee performance include evaluations of nebulous factors such as attitude, work habits, flexibility, job interest, quality of work, and oral communication. These employee characteristics are scored on a 1 to 4 scale by both the employee and the supervisor at annual performance reviews. Many times these evaluations are less than useful or used as a tool to dismiss unpopular employees. They are not useful in ensuring that quality services are efficiently provided to patrons, but they do meet the goal of "employee evaluation" as an afterthought.

The standards for performance explained in this chapter emphasize how to evaluate services for efficiency and quality. Efficient delivery of services is a goal for all NP organizations, and as this goal is applied it provides for organizational accountability. The purpose of establishing standards is to identify better ways to perform the work that needs to be done. Not all work areas need to have detailed standards of performance. Criteria need to be established as to where standards for performance should be applied.

First, if the activity is a non-value-added activity, there is no need to establish standards for these activities. Non-value activities are already wasting the NP's resources, and there is no reason to use more resources evaluating these activities. Such activities need to be eliminated. Second, there are NP activities that simply cannot be evaluated in any effective manner. It is always possible to count visitors coming into an NP organization and call this a standard for performance, but it is not. Visitor counts are so general that they provide little means for specific guidance. Third, more than one measure needs to be used in evaluating performance. Using only one measure will make employees strive to meet that specific performance goal while forsaking other measures that are just as important. . . for example quality. From a cost perspective, standards that are used to evaluate employee performance should, if possible, be based on data that are readily available. There is a cost to collecting new information and those costs should be avoided if possible. Finally, the *rule of the vital few* states that 20 percent of the factors you measure will address 80 percent of the activities that you need to improve. For our purposes, this means that the evaluation methods do not have to be applied throughout the organization.

The performance measures that are described here lend themselves to the development of time and cost performance benchmarks. In a library, such a task would be number of books cataloged or number of books that are shelf read within an hour. Rates can be set for these activities. In a state unemployment agency, similar standards can be established for the number of patrons going on job interviews each day. In an agency for abused women, the standard might deal with the number of cases handled by caseworkers within a specified time period. These job activities lend themselves to the development of specific standards of performance.

SETTING PERFORMANCE STANDARDS

A first step in establishing performance standards is to identify the work activities within a department or other NP work unit. These work activities should have already been identified as non-value-added and value-added activities. As an example, the work functions that are performed in three different responsibility centers in a library are illustrated in figure 6.1. The three responsibility centers are the Technical Services Department and two functional areas within the Reference Department—Library Instruction and Database Search Services. The activities shown for these three centers may vary from one library to another, but they are typical of the functions performed.

Once specific work activities are identified, the standards for performing these activities must be estimated. For example, a standard time allowed for cataloging or recataloging a book in the Technical Services Department can be set. Standards should be measured as reasonably attainable standards instead of ideal standards. Reasonably attainable standards

FIGURE 6.1
Work Activities in Three Library Work Centers

Technical Services
Requisition of library materials
Receive new library materials
Process library materials for shelving
Catalog and recatalog
Maintain inventory awaiting cataloging

Reference Department
Division: Library Instruction
Prepare bibliographic lectures
Prepare general library tours
Deliver bibliographic lectures
Conduct general tours
Division: Database Search Service
Conduct searches
Review requests for new databases
Review adequacy of old databases
Complete paperwork on patron billing
Check invoices from database companies
Select equipment and search aids
Maintain statistics on searches

allow for certain normal inefficiencies, whereas ideal standards assume every task will be performed at 100 percent efficiency all the time—an unattainable goal. Ideal standards assume no allowances for the possible breakdowns of equipment, such as computer problems, or idle time. Attainable standards take into account the level of professional skill of the library's staff as they perform their tasks in an environment that is not perfect.

Standards can be established for the cost of an item, the time required to finish a task, or the quantity of materials to be used in completing the job. Standard costs are predetermined costs per completed unit. They are forecasted and provide a basis against which actual costs can be compared. The standard time allowed to complete a task is the time it should take to complete the actual work that was done. Straightforward, this means that if five books are processed and the standard time is ten minutes per book, the entire process should take fifty minutes. If the actual time to process the five books was fifty-seven minutes, a cost can be attached to the seven-minute unfavorable variance. The standard amount of materials to complete a job can also be specified in terms of cards, sheets of paper, amount of tape, computer time, and so forth, and variances can be determined between the actual amount used and the preset standard. Obviously, it is not necessary to establish standards for every activity in an NP organization, but the use of standards does provide a means to evaluate internal operations. Once a process has been evaluated and improvement made, it may not be necessary to continue to evaluate that same process. For example, standards can be applied on a rotating basis to NP work activities.

The work activities normally performed in the Library Instruction Division are shown in figure 6.1. The activities performed are preparing lectures and tours, delivering lectures, and conducting tours. In table 6.1, the number of times these activities are expected to be performed during the year is estimated, as is the standard time it takes to perform them. The standard can be estimated from an average of previous years' times adjusted to good performance levels, and the measure serves as an attainable time standard for future performance.

The annual labor hours expected to be used during the year are computed by multiplying the number of times the activity is performed times the estimated standard time required to perform the activity. In other words, the amount of time estimated to conduct a library tour is thirty-six minutes; this time allotment is an attainable standard. During the year, it is estimated that fifty tours for incoming freshmen will be necessary. Therefore, the total time allocated to this activity is thirty hours. If the number of tours given should increase to fifty-two, the number of hours to perform this activity should only increase by seventy-two

TABLE 6.1
Annual projected task worksheet

UNIVERSITY LIBRARY

REFERENCE DEPARTMENT—INSTRUCTION DIVISION

BEGINNING PROJECTED WORK ACTIVITY REPORT

PROJECT ACTIVITIES	STANDARD NUMBER OF TIMES	STANDARD TIME REQUIRED PER TASK	LABOR HOURS EXPECTED TO BE USED AT STANDARD TIME (HOURS)
Prepare bibliographic lectures	1	13 hours	13
Prepared general tours	3	4 hours	12
Deliver bibliographic lectures	54	50 minutes	45
Conduct general tours	50	36 minutes	30
Total projected time required to perform work activities			100

minutes (2 x 36 minutes) in order to meet the standard time allotment. If the increase were one hundred minutes, it would mean twenty-eight more minutes were used than was allowed. Once the labor hours are computed for each Instruction Division activity, the total standard time projected to perform all division activities is estimated to be one hundred hours. One hundred labor hours are a good performance standard for the work activities that are performed in the Instruction Division. This is an attainable performance standard for the activities conducted by the division during the year.

Now that performance work standards in hours are established, it is necessary to make a comparison with the actual number of hours used to complete the division's activities that were performed during the year. There is no reason the actual hours would be equal to the hours estimated to be used at the beginning of the budget year. Nor would the actual activity level be the same as initially estimated.

In table 6.2, the actual level of services provided during the year is shown; the number of lectures and tours conducted is higher than the number originally estimated at the beginning of the period. One lecture was prepared, and preparation for general tours was reduced to two. Therefore, the actual services provided, determined at the end of the budget year, are different from the level of services that had been estimated at the beginning of the year. It would be very unusual for the estimated level of services projected at the beginning of a year to turn out to be equal to the actual service level. There are very few clairvoyant budget managers.

In table 6.2, the total amount of time in standard labor hours required to perform each activity is determined. This calculation is based on the standard time allowed (as previously estimated) for each of the activities multiplied times the number of activities performed. For example, sixty bibliographic lectures were presented and each should have taken fifty minutes; therefore the total standard time used on this activity should have been fifty hours.

TABLE 6.2
Annual work tasks based on standard time for completion

UNIVERSITY LIBRARY

REFERENCE DEPARTMENT—INSTRUCTION DIVISION

Year Ended June 30, 20xx

PROJECT ACTIVITIES	NUMBER OF TIMES	STANDARD TIME REQUIRED PER TASK	ANNUAL LABOR HOURS EXPECTED AT STANDARD TIME (STD. HOURS)
Prepare bibliographic lectures	1	13 hours	13.0
Prepared general tours	2	4 hours	8.0
Deliver bibliographic lectures	60	50 minutes	50.0
Conduct general tours	66	36 minutes	39.6
Total standard time required to perform activities			110.6*

*105 actual labor hours were used to complete work activities.

Although table 6.1 showed a total of forty-five hours for this activity that was for a total of fifty-four lectures, not sixty. As the number of lectures increased by six, it would be expected that the time spent on this activity would also increase. Increased time on a task is acceptable as long as it is performed within the standard time allotted. At this point, the actual time used to present sixty bibliographic lectures must be compared with the standard time allowed for sixty lectures—fifty hours. If the actual time used to conduct sixty lectures is significantly more than fifty hours, the reason for the unfavorable time variance needs to be investigated. In reviewing table 6.2, it can be seen that the total standard amount of time allowed to perform the actual activities is 110.6 labor hours. The task reports maintained by library personnel show that only 105 actual labor hours were used in providing the division's services. Although the overall time for performing the four tasks was favorable, each separate work task needs to be reviewed to determine if any one task had a significant unfavorable time variance.

In this example, library personnel performed all four tasks within the standard established and actually used 5.6 hours less than the standard time allowed. As a motivational factor, it may be possible to allow employees who perform their job at better than established standards additional time for personal activity away from work. To make the system fair, steps would have to be taken to ensure employees are keeping accurate records of the time they are spending on work tasks. Of course, such accuracy comes with additional reporting costs.

It would be possible to stop performance evaluation with the information related to the time it takes to complete job functions as shown in figure 6.1 and table 6.1. Such an analysis is better than no analysis. Yet it is possible to incorporate budget dollars with time standards for a more complete analysis.

THERE ALWAYS HAS TO BE A "PLAN B"

For the next step in preparing a performance analysis, assume the year's budget for the Library Instruction Division is shown in table 6.3. It can be seen that the total budget appropriation for the division is $8,400.

To analyze the budget for performance standard setting, the budget appropriations are separated into variable and fixed costs. Only variable and fixed costs are recognized; mixed costs are separated into their fixed and variable components. For example, both salary and maintenance costs can be separated into fixed and variable portions. The salary costs that are fixed are supervisory costs. Supplies and miscellaneous costs are entirely variable. For many NP organizations, the bulk of their budget allocation is composed of fixed costs. The application shown here can still be applied without any difficulties.

The separation of the budget appropriation of $8,400 into its fixed and variable components is shown in figure 6.2. The variable component is shown in the top section of the report ($6,750), and the fixed component ($1,650) is shown in the bottom portion. The variable costs are assumed to be controllable by the division manager. The fixed costs are overhead costs of the division. They are not allocated to this division as uncontrollable overhead from another department (e.g., technology costs), but they are the overhead costs of running the Library Instruction Division.[1]

Once the variable and fixed costs are separated from one another, it is possible to calculate a standard budget rate per hour. Here, the per-unit measure will be based on standard labor hours. Labor hours are used because the division relies entirely on personnel to provide its services. If the job functions in the division did not use a high percentage of labor, it is acceptable to use another activity base as a cost driver. The rate for each labor hour is calculated for each budget line by dividing the appropriation by the one hundred labor hours.

One hundred hours is considered the standard time for good performance as determined in table 6.1 and now used again. The calculation of standard time is made at the beginning of the budget year when the Instruction Division receives its annual appropriation. For illustrative purposes, the actual sequence of calculations was not followed in the chapter.

In figure 6.3, good standard time performance (100 hours) is divided into appropriated budget dollars.[2] The total variable costs are computed to be $67.50 per standard hour, and total fixed costs are $16.50 per standard hour. These are the standard costs per labor hour used to operate the Library Instruction Division.

The analysis shown in figure 6.3 is a combination of standard hours and budget appropriations. The previous analysis of performance standards only included the hours of staff time used to perform their work activities. With the

TABLE 6.3
Budget appropriated for the coming year

UNIVERSITY LIBRARY

REFERENCE DEPARTMENT— INSTRUCTION DIVISION

BUDGET APPROPRIATION
Year Ended June 30, 20xx

BUDGET ITEM	BUDGET APPROPRIATION
Salaries	$5,800
Supplies	1,000
Maintenance	1,400
Miscellaneous	200
Total	$8,400

FIGURE 6.2
Budget Appropriation Separated into Variable and Fixed Components

TOTAL VARIABLE AND FIXED APPROPRIATION

Variable		
Salaries	$4,800	
Supplies & miscellaneous	1,200	
Classroom maintenance	750	
Total variable		$6,750
Fixed		
Supervision	$1,000	
Classroom maintenance	650	
Total fixed		1,650
Total		$8,400

FIGURE 6.3
Standard Rates Based on 100 Hours Needed to Perform Division Activities

CALCULATION OF VARIABLE AND FIXED HOURLY STANDARD RATE

Variable Costs		
Salaries	$4,800/100 1 =	$48.00
Supplies & miscellaneous	$1,200/100 =	12.00
Classroom maintenance	$750/100 =	7.50
Total variable cost per labor hour		$67.50
Fixed Costs		
Supervision	$1,000/100 =	$10.00
Classroom maintenance	$650/100 =	6.50
Total fixed costs per labor hour		$16.50

hourly rate information in figure 6.3 ($48, $12, $7.50, etc.), it is now possible to determine the dollar amount of favorable or unfavorable time difference from standard rates rather than just using over or under time calculations as a measure of performance. This is *Plan B*.

Once the total standard rate for the services is determined in figure 6.3, a budget can be constructed by multiplying the standard rate times the previously determined standard

---

WHY MEN NEVER ASK FOR DIRECTIONS

In the chapter, there are three hourly numbers that are sometimes confusing. They are 105 actual labor hours as recorded by employees, 100 hours that were estimated (table 6.1), and 110.6 hours (table 6.2) that were the standard hours to be used to perform the work.

Let's look at this in another way. Suppose you are planning a road trip. You plan the route to your destination city, and it is 240 miles away. You assume your average (or standard) speed will be 60 miles per hour, and the trip will take 4 hours. This is similar to the 100 hours in our problem which we estimated at the beginning of the budget year. The standard that you have set for your trip is a speed of 60 miles per hour.

You and your wife get in the car. After you are 100 miles down the road your wife looks at the map and tells you that you can save time by taking Route 31 which diagonals across the two roads you intended to follow. When you get to your destination you noticed you had gone 191 miles and it took 3 hours and 45 minutes (225 minutes). This is the actual time like the 105 hours for the Instructional Division.

Going at your standard rate of 60 miles an hour that distance should have taken about 3 hours and 18 minutes (198 minutes). This is similar to the 110.6 in our illustration

You tell your wife she created an unfavorable variance of (225–198) 27 minutes. She tells you she saved you 15 minutes, and YOU are creating an unfavorable variance.

---

hours required to perform the actual activities that had occurred (in the driving example this is 3 hours and 18 minutes). The budget based on standards is illustrated in table 6.4. The standard cost for performing the actual division's activities is shown in table 6.4. The total cost is shown as $9,290.40. This means that the actual cost of providing the division's services should not exceed this amount. In the example, 110.6 hours is used for the variable and fixed components in the illustration. It is assumed that the hours are constant for all activities at 110.6, but this would not necessarily always be true.

In table 6.5, the budget based on standard rates and times (110.6 hours) is compared with the actual costs of running the division which totaled $8,900 as determined from the accounting records. The comparison in table 6.5 is similar to the driving example where twenty-seven minutes were identified as unfavorable. It should be noted that the comparison is not made with the budget appropriated by the board as shown in table 6.3. The purpose here is not to determine if the appropriated budget was over or under spent; rather it is to determine if services were provided within standards of performance established for the division. The comparison with the initial appropriated budget does not take into account the changes that occurred in providing services during the year (e.g., the change in the route in the trip example).

There was an increased level of services provided during the budget year compared with the projected level of services estimated at the beginning of the year.[3] The comparison in table 6.5 takes into account the increased level of actual services and the standard labor hours required to provide those services. It is apparent that the lectures and tours were provided at a cost lower than established standard costs. The actual time used by the staff was 105 labor hours, and the standard time required was 110.6; therefore, the staff provided this level of service more efficiently than the standard time established. This is reflected in the favorable variances. The staff should be commended for their cost performance even though it exceeds the appropriated budget on each budget line.

From a managerial perspective, determining if services are being provided efficiently is more important than whether the legal budget is being exceeded. Unfavorable variances on the report in table 6.5 detect whether library resources are being used inefficiently or wasted. The long-term effect of operating the library inefficiently, assuming limited funding, is likely to be a reduction in services. Yet, the board-approved budget cannot be exceeded. If the legal

TABLE 6.4
Budget costs based on standard hours and standard costs per labor hour

BUDGET ITEM	STANDARD RATE	x	STANDARD HOURS	=	A STANDARD-BASED BUDGET
Variable costs					
Salaries	$48.00	x	110.6	=	$5,308.80
Supplies and miscellaneous	12.00	x	110.6	=	1,327.20
Classroom maintenance	7.50	x	110.6	=	829.50
Fixed costs					
Supervision	$10.00	x	110.6	=	$1,106.00
Maintenance	6.50	x	110.6	=	718.90
Total					$9,290.40

TABLE 6.5
Determining variances using the standard rates and hours and actual incurred budget expenditures

UNIVERSITY LIBRARY

REFERENCE DEPARTMENT—INSTRUCTION DIVISION

BUDGET REPORT*
Year Ended June 30, 20xx

VARIANCE BUDGET ITEM	STANDARD BUDGET DOLLARS (AT STD. HRS.)	ACTUAL BUDGET DOLLARS SPENT (ACTUAL HRS.)	TOTAL VARIANCE FAVORABLE (UNFAVORABLE)
Variable costs			
Salaries	$5,308.80	$5,000.00	$308.80
Supplies and miscellaneous	1,327.20	1,400.00	(72.80)
Classroom maintenance	829.50	800.00	29.50
Fixed costs			
Supervision	$1,106.00	$1,000.00	$106.00
Maintenance	718.90	700.00	18.90
Totals	$9,290.40	$8,900.00	$390.40

*The budget appropriation for the year was $8,400

budget is exceeded, it may mean the director of the library will possibly be fired. In table 6.5, the total variance is $390.40 favorable which looks good, but if the board budget ($8,400) is compared with the actual expenditures ($8,900) there is a $500 unfavorable variance. The latter variance is a legal budget variance, and the former variance is an efficiency variance. For different reasons, it is important to calculate both of them. Although the illustrations here are for the entire fiscal year, computing variance calculations during the budget year is important so that corrective actions can be taken before the end of the year.

Although the budget variances calculated here provide assistance in evaluating efficiency, it would be helpful to have detailed information as to the specific causes of the total favorable variance of $390.40. The total flexible budget variance is composed of the price of assets used, the inefficient or efficient use of those assets, and the total labor hours used in providing services. Determining how these three factors interacted and contributed to the total variance is not be covered here.

YES, BUT WHO IS GOING TO PUT THE "K" IN QUALITY

Another factor that needs to be taken into consideration with such evaluations is the quality of the service provided. Most people have experienced services provided by state government employees who seemed totally oblivious regarding the quality of service they are providing to the public. Can I say "motor vehicles administration" and "quality" in the same sentence? Oh, I just did. Although employees may complete their job functions within accepted time or count criteria, the quality of service they provide is unacceptable. Without additional performance measures beyond time and unit counts, such employees will continue providing low quality services.

One of the most cost effective means used to measure program quality is with opinion surveys of program participants. Many nonprofit organizations use surveys as a method to measure the quality of their programs. If such surveys cannot be administered, then 800 numbers or websites are used to collect information about the service delivery issues. It is important that managers follow up on the information in these reports if any deficiencies in service quality are to be corrected.

Other methods can be used to measure program quality. As programs are presented it may be possible to have a staff member act as an observer of the program's delivery. Their objective would be to determine how to make helpful improvements in the organization and presentation of the programs. Another method is to conduct short interviews with patrons and ask them directly how they view the program. Such interviews are called exit interviews. The qualitative information collected allows the NP organization to begin to form an understanding of the population it is serving and also possibly help explain why some of its budget costs are beginning to change as its patron and donor base changes.

OK . . . TELL ME, WHICH ONE COUNTS?

The Sustainable Forestry Initiative's recently revised standards are based on 14 core principles, 20 objectives, 39 performance measures and 114 indicators, all of which are applied universally. The SFI core principles include, "Forest productivity and health," "Protection of water resources," and "Protection of biological diversity," as well as "Avoidance of controversial sources including illegal logging in offshore fiber sourcing."[4]

SUMMARY

Methods used to compute standards of performance can become complicated, and they should be used where the additional information is worth the added effort. They do not have to be used over the entire organization. It is possible to adopt these methods for an area of operations where it is believed efficiencies can be introduced if more analysis is provided. It should also be remembered that methods such as these should be adopted with those NP activities that add value to the organization's mission, and not with non-value-added activities.

The budget reports in the chapter have illustrated that the budget appropriation may be exceeded by a department or agency, but the reason may not be inefficiency. It may be due to the fact that services were provided at a higher level with the appropriated budget resources. It is possible to uncover this relationship when standards for performance are established for actual service levels and compared with actual resource usage. Once these reports begin to be prepared, they provide managers with a different view on their operations that allows them to make managerial decisions using a new perspective.

NOTES

1. These costs are not directly controllable by the division manager. Variance computed based on fixed costs need to be reviewed, but the manager should not be held accountable for unfavorable results.

2. Although total fixed costs will not change over the period, this calculation for fixed costs will show that as the volume of services performed increases, the fixed cost per unit decreases. Therefore, the fixed cost per unit is understood to vary if the standard labor hours to complete division activities change.

3. If the projected budget at the beginning of the year was compared with the actual amounts spent, all variances would be unfavorable. This result is only due to the increased level of service provided by the division and not due to a deficiency in performance. Figure 6.8 clearly illustrates that the division is meeting its performance goals.

4. Monte Paulsen, "EcoGroup's Trade Complaint Targets Wood Certifier," *Tyee*, March 16, 2010, http://thetyee.ca/News/2010/03/16/EcoGroupComplaint.

SEVEN

MANAGERS NEED TO MEASURE UP, TOO

Leaders get out in front and stay there by raising the standards by which they judge themselves—and by which they are willing to be judged.

Fredrick W. Smith

If an NP organization is faced with a budget crisis, top executives and managers are crucial in reducing the effect of appropriation cuts on the viability of the organization. The leaders of NP organizations have to set the path for the organization, and they need to ensure that it stays on course. If they have set fundraising as their goal, they need to have defined benchmarks against which such goals are measured. If the goal is to cut back on costs while maintaining services, then that goal also needs to have set benchmarks to ensure achievement.

Although some NP leaders may be able to face these issues without a plan, most NP managers need an outline and guidelines for focusing on the issues. The more serious the problems are facing the NP, the more important it is have an outline and forecasts for future changes. These guidelines and plans adopt a strategic viewpoint. If any NP is going to be facing closure in the next week, setting a strategic plan will not change that outcome.

Everyone needs to be evaluated.

Certain employees can be subjected to time standards. On the other hand, managers whose activities are not subjected to counts must be evaluated from a strategic perspective. Without a doubt, these performance measures are many times very subjective as it is difficult to see a direct relationship between the manager's job performance and outcomes. Yet, there are solutions to this correlation problem.

A FEW BASICS FIRST

There are general criteria of evaluation necessary for all performance evaluation systems. First, they should provide current data in a timely manner. If the feedback on performance objectives is out of date, it is useless to the manager, who cannot take effective corrective actions. Therefore, timeliness is an important criterion.

Data provided on performance should be shown in a comparative format in order for the manager to evaluate the level of change from previous periods. This provides clear answers to the question, *How well am I doing?* When these comparisons are made, an external standard is more useful than an internal benchmark. Internal comparisons only mean that results are better than last year, but last year's result may be so poor an improvement means little. Comparisons against external standards when possible make for fairer evaluations.

Performance evaluation has a direct effect on behavior and should be carefully considered before being implemented. If a performance objective is established that is too "ideal" or unreachable, it can seriously decrease employee motivation. Although it is acceptable to establish performance within attainable standards, the establishment of unattainable objectives only causes decreased employee morale as employees realize that they cannot achieve the objective—so why bother? Another factor to consider is using a mixture of performance criteria and not stressing just one evaluator. Without a mixture of performance criteria for the evaluation, a manager's behavior will be directed at achieving success on a narrow range of evaluators, which may have unintended consequences that are detrimental to the NP organization.

If performance data are self-reported, care must be taken to ensure employees do not fudge data to make their performance look good. For example, if a Circulation Department is not sending overdue notices on a timely basis, then a way to correct the situation is to count the number of overdue notices sent. To fudge this data and get a "good" count on this evaluator, the Circulation Department sends overdue notices to patrons who still have several days left to hold borrowed materials. Essentially, the data have been tweaked to meet the evaluation criteria.[1]

Another factor that needs to be considered is the culture of the NP organization. Many of the measures suggested here deal with the reporting of numbers and using numbers or their ratios to evaluate employee and managerial performance. Yet, such an approach may be totally foreign to some managers and NP organizations. These organizations will consider the application and implementation of the methods suggested here as an imposition on their managerial decision making. There is no answer to this issue. The methods that are suggested here are being used to help organizations as they face budget reductions, and consequently their operations have to be defined and evaluated using numerical data.

Timeliness of data, comparative data, attainable standards, a mixture of performance, and reliable data are some of the primary considerations in establishing any performance criteria for managerial control and goal achievement.

OK . . . LET THE COUNTS BEGIN

Many NP managers evaluate their performance through counts of activities such as number of patrons, number of cases completed, number of job placements, total amount of money raised, number of potholes filled, and time required to answer an incoming call. Except for response time, increases in counts are considered good and decreases are bad. Unfortunately, such counts are usually too short term in nature, and they use a one-way focus that prevents meaningful strategic evaluations.

Activity counts are the simplest method that can be used for evaluating managerial performance. When this method is used, it is a gauge of workload incurred in a work unit, or department. For example, in a Reference Department, workload numbers can be provided about the number of reference questions answered as well as periodical or website usage. In a social welfare agency, the number of completed cases can be counted. Such data provide information about the demand for services but little else. This information is helpful, but it does not provide information as to whether strategic initiatives are being met.

Measures of efficiency have been explained in the previous chapter, and they are often and unfortunately used to measure executive or managerial performance. Efficiency measures weigh the amount of resources used to achieve outcomes. Many performance measures established to assess efficiency are based on cost-per-item calculations. When there is a decrease in the cost per item of output, it is interpreted as an increase in the efficiency of operations. In a social welfare agency, such a measure might be the cost-per-client. Efficiency measures are better measures of performance than simple workload counts, but they provide little strategic guidance for a manager.

Effectiveness is separate from efficiency as a performance measure. It is based on the extent to which instituted policy guidelines are achieved. These policies can include objectives that are to be attained in the future, such as yearly service objectives. These objectives should be established with enough specificity that they are truly measurable as performance criteria. Many times NP objectives are not specific enough to have a serious impact on changing behavior. For example, a policy goal of a 2 percent increase in patrons served is not as specific as the departmental goal of a 2 percent increase in flu shots administered from November to February.

Administrative input into the success of an organization's goals needs to be measured. Such evaluations should be oriented toward long-term strategic initiatives. Administrative outcome measurement is essentially a series of program effectiveness measures with a long-term, mission-based orientation.

WE GOOD . . . OH YEAH!

Excellus Board Voted Itself a 37 Percent Pay Raise

The directors of Excellus voted to raise their pay by 37 percent last year after a consultant hired by the insurer determined they were underpaid. The raises for the 17 outside directors came at the same time the nonprofit insurer lost money on its operations and cut the pay of its top executives.

The same year, Excellus increased health insurance rates on average 8 percent. For 2010, the insurer raised its rates an average of 8.8 percent. Both years, some customers saw substantially higher rate increases.[2]

IS THINKING TWO DAYS AHEAD A LONG-TERM STRATEGY?

Due to the long-term nature required for the evaluation of NP managers, such performance criteria are often difficult to develop. Many times subjective criteria are used because no one has a better method of evaluation. Such subjective methods of performance evaluation are dependent on what the boss thinks about a manager and this evaluation method leapfrogs up the organization chain all the way to the board of directors. Another method is the five-point opinion scale. An immediate supervisor or the board rates managers on such factors such as job knowledge, collegiality, work habits, creating employee motivation, and dependability. Unfortunately, these rating scales are only subjective evaluations transferred to a paper format. The use of such an approach can achieve a lot of scattered goals, but the obvious problem is there is no focused long-term approach. Further, it brings the fairness of the evaluation into question for others in the organization.

Evaluative measures for administrators need to be more transparent and less subjective. Yet, the work activities of administrators are not highly structured, and there are imperfect data collected about long-term program success.

One method that can be applied to assessing administrative performance and relating it to long-term strategic initiatives is the balanced scorecard (BSC). The BSC provides the tools for administrators to tie financial and nonfinancial performance evaluation into the mission and strategic initiatives of the organization. Administrative success in achieving those goals serves as a means of performance evaluation.

PUT THEIR FEET TO THE FIRE!

When is a respite turned into goldbricking and slacking? There is the story of an NP director who took an hour each afternoon to do "reading and paperwork" in his office. During this time, he shut his office door and left word that he was not to be disturbed. His staff assumed he was conducting organizational business until one wintry afternoon he burst out of his office screaming with his shoes smoking and burning. He had fallen asleep with his feet on an electric heater.

A common theme for usage of the BSC is to develop a selected series of performance targets for evaluating financial, patron, internal processes, and employee learning and growth measures into a mixture that allows the organization to achieve its strategic initiatives. Financial measures relate to the traditional monetary ratios that are used to evaluate an NP. For example, the implementation of a 10 percent budget cut could be a financial target. The assessment of patron satisfaction with services provided by the NP is the next area to be evaluated. For internal processes, performance is focused on those areas where the NP does comparatively better in providing services than other organizations. Internal processes identify the area(s) of strategic direction for the organization. Learning and growth measurements relate to employees and their development. For the organization to successfully achieve its long-term initiatives, its employees must be adequately trained and skilled, for example.

These measures have to be tied together in a way that allows for success in one area to support success in another area at the same time. As the BSC is a very open approach, it also allows strategic initiatives to be communicated to all levels in the NP organization. Figure 7.1 introduces the matrix relationship between these four performance areas. The coordination of these four areas within a set of objectives, measures, target goals, and initiatives is vital for the overall success of the organization. It can also be used to focus on managerial performance when financial viability of the organization becomes questionable due to budget cuts.

The basic outline in figure 7.1 links each BSC objective (in column one) together to support one overall mission statement goal. For example, the mission statement goal may be "to increase the number of patrons using our services by 5 percent during the next year" or "targeting a particular demographic group for expanded services" such as teenagers or the retired. Each such mission statement goal requires a *separate* outline of BSC objectives, performance measures, targets, and initiatives as shown in figure 7.1.

The target column presents a benchmark that is to be achieved. The administrator's performance is evaluated on how successfully he achieves the target goal. The initial initiative column shows the first steps the administrator is taking to reach his target goal. An administrative evaluation based on the achievement of specific target goals is less subjective than a 1-to-5 opinion survey used to evaluate "dependability" as an administrative characteristic.

Even without defining objectives, performance measures, targets, or initial initiatives for figure 7.1, it still can be seen that once these factors are selected, their coordination with one another becomes implicit. One identified objective in the BSC has one performance

FIGURE 7.1
Basic Outline for One Mission Statement
Objective under the BSC

MISSION GOAL: To increase the number of patrons using our services by 5% during the next year.

PERSPECTIVE	OBJECTIVE	PERFORMANCE MEASURE	TARGET GOAL	INITIAL INITIATIVE
Financial				
Patron				
Internal Processes				
Learning & Growth				

measure and target goal for each of the following areas: financial, patron, internal processes, and learning and growth. The BSC target goal is a ratio or nonfinancial goal that needs to be achieved by the administrator. As the number of objectives is expanded, the performance measures are expanded by a multiple of four. For example, four separate objectives would require sixteen performance measures. It becomes clear that the list of BSC objectives and performance measures can quickly become unmanageable. Objectives must be judiciously selected.

As NP organizations face continuing budget crises, an important objective for developing a BSC is financial viability. Using the BSC allows managers to become aware of organizational processes that contribute to long-term organizational viability. The starting point for using the BSC in NP management begins with the mission statement and the objectives that flow from it. Once incorporated into the BSC, the future four target goals are later evaluated as to whether they have been achieved.

As previously stated, the administrative performance is difficult to trace because manager's activities are related to achieving long-term initiatives. The remainder of this chapter presents examples as to how the BSC can be used to evaluate administrative performance and the implementation of goals into annual administrative contracts for performance.

THE BSC, BUDGET CUTS, AND ADMINISTRATOR'S PERFORMANCE

The BSC can be used to help when NP organizations are faced with budget cuts, but it is a long-term strategy that cannot be implemented two days before the lights are turned off. When faced with a budget reduction, the NP manager can use the BSC to identify required performance measures and target goals in each of the four areas: (1) financial, (2) patron, (3) internal processes, and (4) learning and growth. Specific performance measures need to be selected for each area and the NP manager evaluated based on the achievement of those goals. These specific goals are selected because the NP manager can affect their outcome.

An illustration of such an approach is provided in figure 7.2 for the Perry Library. The Perry Library is faced with a deep reduction in its budget appropriation. In each of the four areas, the Perry Library has selected an initiative for its administrator that will tie managerial efforts together as they are implemented. Only the first initiative is a financial goal. The other initiatives are related to patron satisfaction, internal core process where the library is trying to make a change, and employee goals.

The NP administrator's evaluation for the coming period is partially based on obtaining the results under the target column. These target goals are a 10 percent budget dollar cost reduction per patron; maintaining a 4.0 average on the patron survey; ensuring one letter requesting support is sent to each local official, state and federal elected official; and ensuring that each employee is involved in one community outreach activity during the year. A report is filed with the board on the successful outcome of these performance goals at the end of the year.

FIGURE 7.2
Adapting the BSC for Budget Reduction and the Performance Evaluation of Administrators

ADMINISTRATIVE GOAL: Seeking community support while cutting the budget

PERRY LIBRARY'S BSC

PERSPECTIVE	OBJECTIVE	PERFORMANCE MEASURE	TARGET GOAL	INITIAL INITIATIVE
Financial	Reduce NP budget	Cost per patron	−10%	Identify non-value-added activities for reduction
Patron	Prevent deterioration of patron satisfaction with services	Survey responses	4.0 average score on opinion responses related patron satisfaction using a 5-point scale	Provide education to patrons about the exact nature of required budget crisis and how the NP organization is dealing with them
Internal Processes	Seek grant support for additional funding	Number of letters written to local, state, and Congressional representatives and leaders for grant support	One letter to each local, state, and Congressional leader	Build political support base for grant funding
Learning & Growth	Employee/ Community outreach	Number of outreach activities per employee	One outreach activity per employee	Employee outreach into the community to help build a strong community support base as the NP is faced with budget and service reductions

Using an instrument that allows for evaluation based on specific ratios, instead of patron counts, allows for an evaluation of the administrator's actions against agreed-upon standards. It would be expected that such ratios would change as the annual conditions facing the NP changed.

In figure 7.2, the objectives tie together with one another. While the financial objective is the reduction of the budget, the internal processes are used to try to establish the groundwork for grant applications. The grant application process is successfully achieved with external political support, and the library is trying to build that support by initially sending out letters to politicians who may be able to influence the granting process. Such activities would have to be followed up with additional network-building activity.

To have the library's patrons better understand the financial situation the library is facing, the library director will expand efforts to educate the public about mandated budget cuts and the effect it will have on library services. Any reduction in patron services will be closely tied in with an explanation of the budget reductions the library is facing. Service reduction will not be unilaterally announced by the library without first educating the public as to the reasons for the reductions and seeking their input.

Employees are involved in budget reduction efforts by helping to raise public awareness of the library's interaction with the community. The purpose of these outreach activities is to help the community and build a reservoir of community goodwill. If budget reductions become more severe, it may be necessary to release employees. At that time, the library may have to call on volunteer staff and other support from the community to keep the library open.

The performance indicators for the four areas—financial, patron, internal processes, and learning and growth—vary with the mission of the organization as well as those internal processes in which the organization excels. Therefore, there is no acceptable list of evaluators that will provide for the requirements of each library or NP organization. With this qualification, a list of overall library—not departmental—evaluators is provided in figure 7.3. These evaluators are examples of ratios, but they are not coordinated with each other in any manner. The best way to view figure 7.3 is as a vertical list under each heading.

The list contains evaluators that lag performance. If possible, it is best to have evaluators that lead performance trends. For example, survey responses are more likely to provide leading indications of future trends than are metrics taken off the financial report. A timely analysis from a survey will show potential changes in patrons' attitudes beginning to occur, whereas financial ratios from the last year only show what has happened in the past, not future trends. It should also be noted that these measures appear as surrogates for the administrative performance that is being evaluated.

In figure 7.3, the financial measures are directed toward evaluating the overall viability of the library. Variance measures are included under the financial heading to determine how well the overall finances of the library are managed. Each NP organization would have specific strategic initiatives developed under its mission statement.

The measures under internal processes in figure 7.3 are general illustrative measures. For example, two of the measures review the trend in administrative costs as a percentage of total appropriations and from the number of employees administered. The actual costs considered to be part of the "administrative costs" category would have to be determined by each library.

Many of the patron and employee measures indicate how these groups view the organization as well as provide indications of the trends in those areas. All comparisons should be among external benchmarks, first, or previous periods to identify the direction of any data trends.

FIGURE 7.3

Generalized BSC Evaluators for a Variety of Mission Statement Goals

FINANCIAL	PATRON	INTERNAL PROCESSES	LEARNING & GROWTH
Governmental budget dollars received divided by patrons	Number and trend of patrons using NP services	Administrative costs/total appropriation	Hours of technology training per employee
Increase in budgeted funding from previous year	Satisfaction index scores on patron service (satisfaction survey)	Average time for decision making in days	Share of employees below the age of 40
Total cost of operations divided by patrons	Number and trend of complaints	New books/total collection	Satisfaction index scores on employee work satisfaction survey
Total cost of operations divided by total books in collection	Change in patron demographics, i.e., income level, marital status	Dollars spent on new technology	Number and type of suggestions in employee suggestion box
Variances from budgeted amounts	Number and trend of overdue library books	Administrative cost per employee	Number of part-time and temporary employees/total employees

WHO WOULD NOTICE A LITTLE LACK OF MAINTENANCE?

Whenever there are budget cuts called for in an NP, administrators attempt to make the cuts as invisible as possible. Yet, these cuts may not be in the best long-term interests of the NP organization. Such "invisible" cuts do not affect the performance evaluation of the NP administrator because they are not reported. One of the most common methods of making "invisible" cuts during budget reductions is to cut maintenance on the NP's facilities. Even when there are no budget cuts, NP administrators see dollars spent on the maintenance of facilities as a readily available source of cash. Therefore, one of the most common methods to "find" funds when budgets are cut is to defer the maintenance of facilities. These cuts can go unnoticed for long periods of time, but eventually funds must be provided to make up for years of neglect. These funds are used for extensive renovation or the rebuilding of prematurely deteriorated facilities. It is possible to use an adaption of the BSC to clearly report the effect of such decisions and make them visible to the NP's stakeholders.

Deferred maintenance occurs from the intentional reduction in facility support and repair. The level of deferred maintenance required to keep facilities in good operating order can be measured. The evaluation of deferred maintenance provides an indication of purposeful administrative action to pay for the present by robbing the future. In the traditional financial reports, deferred maintenance goes unreported. Yet, when deliberate administrative actions, such as these, are taken to manipulate funding, they should be identified. NP managers need to be held accountable for these decisions.

If facility maintenance is inadequate to the point of deterioration, a question arises as to the manager's ability to raise supplemental funds to make up for the accelerated payments required to rebuild deteriorated facilities. An administrator could have a benefactor willing to provide these monies at a future date so that premature obsolescence and deterioration of facilities is not a serious problem. So, improper maintenance may be compensated for by a generous benefactor . . . possibly.

The first step in evaluating performance outcomes related to deferred maintenance is to determine the difference between the expenditures that should be made for proper maintenance of assets and the actual amount expended for maintenance. The goal is to determine if there are shortfalls that are going to require the early replacement of physical facilities. Information from vendors is usually available regarding the amount of yearly maintenance charges needed to properly maintain physical assets. If this information is not available from vendors, the cost of proper maintenance of buildings, vehicles, and equipment can be estimated.[4]

Using these estimates and the actual maintenance expenditures—as recorded in the accounting records—a deferred maintenance charge can be calculated. The charge is a variance between actual maintenance expenditures and the expenditures recommended in vendor maintenance guides. If less is expended than recommended, the difference is recognized as curtailed maintenance expenditures.

If there is a shortfall in budget monies for facility maintenance—planned or unplanned—administrators need to secure additional funding from donations or grants for maintenance or asset replacement. If the administrator, who is responsible for inadequate maintenance, does not have the skill to attract additional funds, then their performance evaluation should reflect their inability to perform.

In figure 7.4, a report similar to the BSC shows the interaction of three measures related to deferred maintenance and managerial assessment. If the level of deferred maintenance is found to be increasing (row one, column two), it needs to reflect negatively on the administrator's performance evaluation. It would be expected that successful administrators could counter this effect by finding other sources of funding for maintenance. Rows two (external funding) and three (supplemental support) in figure 7.4 are used to track other funding

USMMA FACILITIES "AT A TIPPING POINT"

The condition of the physical plant of the U.S. Merchant Marine Academy, Kings Point, N.Y., has "reached a tipping point."

"Academic and support buildings were inadequately maintained, basic structural elements of some buildings were failing, electrical and plumbing support had deteriorated, and engineering laboratories were outdated. The pier facilities, dining hall, athletics complex, and two of the dormitories, were in particularly poor condition," says the report.

Consistent with the sustainment, restoration and modernization approach to life-cycle facility management Merchant Marine Academy funding should be restructured to provide for three separate funding streams: facilities maintenance, equipment, and capital improvements.[3]

FIGURE 7.4

Using the BSC for Deferred Maintenance Recognition and Funding Support

ADMINISTRATIVE GOAL: Maintain Facility Functionality

OBJECTIVE	PERFORMANCE MEASURE	TARGET	INITIAL INITIATIVE
Maintain Facility Assets	Recommended maintenance dollars less current maintenance in budgeted dollars = deferred charge	Zero difference in the measure	Request for added maintenance expenditures in budget if shortfall is due to budget cuts
Increase External Funding	External funding dollars received	Annual dollars of external funding equal to 5% of total budget for asset replacement	Formulation of a community advisory committee including community leaders for generating supplemental support
Supplemental Support for Maintenance	Dollars of external supplemental support/deferred maintenance charge	Should be equal to one	Formulation of a community advisory committee including community leaders for generating supplemental support

sources. This funding needs to be obtained outside the annual budget appropriation. If the NP administrators are reducing maintenance, their overall performance is evaluated based on how successful they are in obtaining other funding. In order to make up for a reduction in maintenance and asset deterioration, the minimum increase in external funding is 5 percent of the total budget. The minimum target ratio for supplemental funding (row 3, column 3) when deferred maintenance is occurring is shown in figure 7.4 as a target measure of one. This relationship means that each dollar of under-spending on recommended maintenance is being made up for with a dollar of supplemental support. An administrator who is cutting maintenance and cannot get an additional budget appropriation (row 1, column 4) knows it is necessary to make up for the cuts with external or supplemental funding.

If the NP administrators meet their budget reduction target through cutting maintenance costs, it will have long-term negative impacts on the organization. As these budget cuts are implemented, it is important to ensure that they do not fly under the radar. Successful budget cutting does not mean crippling the organization for years in the future. Using an adapted BSC chart will help uncover these manipulative techniques. The evaluation of the NP managers is dependent on how successful they are in overcoming these "invisible" budget cuts by raising supplemental funding to cover the deferred maintenance deficit.

In the current curtailed funding environment, a manager may have to make a choice between drastically cutting maintenance or services, but regardless, the fact that maintenance has been cut should not go unreported. The current savings in maintenance expenditures may result in unanticipated and accelerated increases in future expenditures to make up for years of deficits.

Even without budget cuts, it may be possible to curtail maintenance expenditures and use maintenance monies for new initiatives in the NP organization that make an administrator appear to be a dynamic leader. In these cases, the director may be able to find a new position before the deterioration becomes apparent. The reporting system should raise red flags to make the board and other interested parties aware of the situation occurring through such contriving behavior.[5]

. . . AND THE SCORES ARE IN

When the BSC is used as a means to evaluate higher-level NP administrators, eventually the results of the evaluation must be compared with the BSC target goals. At that time, the administrator is evaluated on how well agreed-upon targets were achieved. There is some subjectivity to these evaluations. Yet, if the target is a 10 percent budget reduction with non-value activities cut out first, and the administrator made a 10 percent across-the-board cut, they should be rated less than adequate on this target goal. If the target is to reduce administrative cost per employee by 3 percent and the administrative cost per employee has increased, then again the administrator's evaluation should reflect the inability to reach an agreed-upon goal.

The use of a BSC involves more closely monitoring administrative activities than does a 1-to-5 point opinion scale that is used as a generalized annual performance measure. It means the supervisors doing the rating have to base it on hard data rather than their "gut" feelings. The data upon which an administrator is being rated are transparent to everyone viewing the assessment.

When the BSC is used to evaluate performance, the time period for each target does not have to be the same. It is not necessary to try to force every evaluation target into a one-year time period, for example. It is acceptable to use a shorter time period for some target goals and even extend the time period beyond a one-year time frame for others. In the latter case, there would have to be progress reports completed and matched with other evaluations.

An important decision when using the BSC is to determine how many target goals to use in evaluating a specific administrator. One mission statement goal increases the target goals by four. It is suggested here that the administrator should be typically working on no more than eight strategic targets at any one time. Depending on the nature of the targets, it may be possible to expand them to twelve, but performance measures and targets need to be selected with care. The combination of evaluators should not be so extensive as to scatter the focus of administrative efforts beyond reasonable expectations.

The target goals do not have to be equally weighted in the evaluation. If it is believed that certain targets need to be emphasized more than others, they can be weighted by a multiple of the others. Weighting will cause the NP administrator to understand the areas the board or other supervisor believes are vital to the long-term success of the organization.

Even though the BSC is being presented as a managerial technique to use in the evaluation of higher-level administrators, it does not have to be used as the single means of assessment. Other measures can be used in conjunction with the BSC as long as they complement the achievement of strategic objectives facing the NP.

GET IT IN WRITING

If it is agreed that administrative outcomes can be objectively measured and evaluated, then it is possible to contract for administrative performance and outcomes. Successful performance is based on how well contracted outcomes are achieved. Performance outcomes can be established with a BSC and used for managerial evaluation throughout an NP's administrative organizational chart.

A contract for long-term performance should be agreed upon by the administrator and his or her superior. The contract should have specific outcomes against which actual performance can be compared. Evaluated administrators should exercise authority to influence their contracted performance outcomes as they cannot be evaluated against outcomes over which they have no control. Through a system of contracts at all managerial levels, goals can be harmonized and tied to an NP's mission. As administrators explain these goals to managers and staff within the nonprofit hierarchy, it is possible to develop a cooperative network of interacting BSC objectives.

A criterion of contracts for performance is that the outcomes are controllable, long-term in nature, and specified in enough detail to determine whether they have been achieved. The administrator must be given enough leeway with the organization's resources to use them in the most efficient manner possible. This latter requirement means that very tight restrictions on the use of funds will have to be eased. Managers must have full control over resources allocated to them. In this way, they have responsibility for achieving contracted outcomes as well as the means to achieve them. Such a flexible use of resources may not be acceptable in NP organizations structured around a hierarchical management system.

The purpose of contracting for performance is to help remove partiality in the evaluation of administrative performance. The contract provides a clear and realistic definition of the job that an administrator is requested to perform and outlines their accountability for long-term objectives. It also gives that administrator the ability to change the resource mix in a manner that best achieves the defined outcomes. Good management cannot concentrate operational decisions in the short-term. Short-term managing needs to be supplemented with strategic objectives. Success in achieving only short-term goals does not lead to success with long-term outcomes. It is good to have short-term goals, but the organization cannot successfully function without a long-term strategy. Contracting for performance is one method for achieving an organization's strategic objectives.

SUMMARY

Administrative evaluations are difficult without a concrete definition of performance. They cannot be measured as counts or cost-per-unit basis. Further, it is difficult to establish short-term goals for such administrators that are directly related to strategic long-term initiatives. The BSC provides a means to make administrative evaluation more defined, less subjective, and more strategic.

In the chapter, the BSC is adapted for administrative performance evaluation. Traditionally, the BSC is a cooperative process when it is applied to the entire organization, but here it is playing a more limited role. As such, its normal cooperative process is restricted to administrative contractual development.

The wholesale cutting of every budget line can result in a destructive downward spiral for the organization. When an NP organization is faced with a budget crisis, it is possible to use the BSC to ensure that the best long-term decisions are being made as budget cuts are implemented. One example described in the chapter was to prevent the long-term deterioration of the NP's physical facilities, but there are other examples of these applications. The BSC allows for a defined response to try to reduce the effects on patron services and long-term organizational viability.

Administrative performance can be measured in terms of preset goals established through a series of organization-wide contracts. These contracts define long-range achievement goals. They allow for an organization-wide BSC orientation and continuity toward achieving the organization's mission.

REFERENCES

Kaplan, R. S., and D. P. Norton. *The Balanced Scorecard: Translating Strategy into Action.* Boston: Harvard Business School Press, 1996.

Kaplan, R. S., and D. P. Norton. *The Strategy-Focused Organization: How Balanced Scorecard Companies Thrive in the New Business Environment.* Boston: Harvard Business School Press, 2001.

Zweizig, D., and E. J. Rodger. *Output Measures for Public Libraries: A Manual of Standardized Procedures.* Chicago: American Library Association, 1987.

NOTES

1. A correction to this problem would be to compare overdue notices with the number of overdue books recorded in the records.

2. James T. Mulder, "Excellus Board Voted Itself a 37 Percent Pay Raise," *Post-Standard*, March 16, 2010, www.syracuse.com/news/index.ssf/2010/03/excellus_board_voted_itself_a.html.

3. "USMMA Facilities at a Tipping Point," *MarineLog*, March 11, 2010, www.marinelog.com/DOCS/NEWSMMIX/2010mar00115.html.

4. In certain cases, NP managers may decide the only way they can receive funding for new assets is by allowing old assets to conspicuously deteriorate. The managerial concept is that a public eyesore is more likely to receive budget attention.

5. The typical accounting system also does not record information about deferred maintenance charges. One way to collect deferred maintenance data is with the performance audit. With a performance audit, information can be collected to determine if there is a shortfall in maintenance expenditures. The board of directors of a library can request that a performance audit be conducted.

EIGHT

LOSING IT ALL TO FRAUD

Accountants don't currently learn what motivates fraudulent conduct, how to spot the signals, how to prevent fraud from occurring and much more. As it stands now, auditors are fighting a war without being taught how to recognize the enemy. Until that changes, expect more heavy casualties.

Joseph T. Wells, *SmartPros*

There are some frauds so well conducted that it would be stupidity not to be deceived by them.

Charles Caleb Colton, *Lacon*

Financial fraud can occur when an NP's recordkeeping is honest and yet a fraud is committed. An example would be inflated invoice prices combined with kickbacks to vendors. Fraud may also occur when fraudulent recordkeeping is an issue. In this case, it means an employee is keeping fraudulent accounting records in order to commit a financial fraud; an example would be stealing cash and covering it up with fraudulent entries in the NP's books. These are two different situations that will be discussed in the chapter.

Before dealing with the types of fraud that can occur in an NP, let's consider the role of the NP's auditor. When an NP receives an audit opinion from CPAs that makes no reference to frauds or theft, it does not mean that there is no ongoing fraud or theft within the NP. The role of the auditor in detecting significant financial fraud has been expanded in recent years, but it is not the job of the auditor to search for fraud. The auditor has been hired to comment on the financial statement prepared by management to ensure that these reports are following accepted accounting standards. If a significant fraud should be happened upon in the audit, it will be reported, but the auditors are not searching for fraudulent behavior. Responsibility for the stewardship of NP resources rests with the administrators and board. An NP financial collapse due to the theft of resources or fraudulent recordkeeping is one of the most serious indictments of managerial control over its stewardship of an NP's resources.

Unfortunately NP organizations provide a fertile ground for the commitment of financial frauds due to a lack of internal controls. Internal control is a system of financial and nonfinancial practices followed to safeguard an organization's resources. Internal controls can deal with the resolutions passed by the board or they can deal with the procedures followed in issuing credit cards to NP executives. In NPs, there is a general culture of trust among employees, and that culture allows unethical employees an opening to commit fraud. In addition, there are a limited number of employees to ensure that internal controls are properly executed. These two conditions are the main reason for the large number of successful frauds and thefts that occur in NPs.

YOU HAD ME AT "INTERNAL CONTROL"

There are many internal control techniques that are only the concern of the accountant. Still, NP managers should be aware of the fraud risks to their organization from weak or nonexistent internal controls. These risks include loss of assets, termination of employees, law suits, increased insurance costs, loss of reputation, and possible financial crisis or collapse of the NP. Without a good system of internal control, the NP's resources are at risk of being lost. Any NP manager who is concerned with the efficiency and effectiveness of operations is also interested in knowing the NP's assets are not being misappropriated.

Will a system of internal controls stop fraud and the theft of assets? The answer is: "Definitely not." Internal controls can be overridden by managers or ignored. Will internal controls help to prevent the loss of assets? Yes. So, it could be worse without the application of internal controls.

Certain specific standards are in effect when internal control practices are implemented. These internal control practices are commonsense applications used to protect an NP's resources. First, it is important to have competent and trustworthy personnel. Today, a background check should be conducted for any employee who is responsible for dispersing cash or other spending authority. Such a background check will reveal any past financial irregularities or other issues. An internal control policy requires that access to valuable assets such as paintings, other artwork, artifacts, and historical documents are controlled. These safeguards need to be periodically reviewed to determine if they are being enforced.

One weak internal control area for NPs is in the segregation of job functions when financial functions are performed. The segregation of duties means that job functions are separated in such a manner that if one employee commits a fraud another employee will become aware of the fraud. The segregation of job functions makes it more difficult to commit a fraud without being detected. For example, if one employee is responsible for entering transactions into the books, issuing purchase orders, the receipt of ordered goods, and making bank reconciliations, it is very easy for that person to falsify records without being detected. If these business activities are separated so that at least two employees are involved, it becomes more difficult to implement the fraud. One employee should be responsible for approving checks, another for receiving cash, and a third employee should be responsible for making bank reconciliations. All checks above a set amount should have dual signatures on the check. There needs to be a similar policy for purchases above a specific dollar level. In the latter cases, the practice works as long as the employee does not falsify numerous individual transactions below the cutoff level. The limited staff in most NPs makes it difficult to adequately segregate employee's job functions.

If an NP has fidelity bonded employees, it still may not help. When employees are bonded, it means that an insurance company has provided a guarantee, for a fee, that if the bonded employee steals a valuable asset the loss can be recovered from the insurance company. As with most insurance policies, there are caveats. If the NP has not maintained "reliable" accounting practices, the insurance company can refuse to pay for the loss. Reliable accounting practices mean good internal control over resources.

One way to overcome internal control problems with a small staff is to enforce job rotation and vacation scheduling or outsource financial functions. Job rotation ensures that no one employee remains forever responsible for key financial functions in the NP organization.

When one long-time employee refuses to take a vacation, NP managers should be suspicious, not overjoyed, that they do not have to pay for vacation days. Vacation schedules need to be enforced. If there are discrepancies in the records, the temporary replacement employee is likely to detect the fraud. Outsourcing of specific financial functions such as payroll help to segregate duties when there is little other choice.

The NP can seek help from internal auditors if there are suspicions of fraud. Most NPs are part of a larger governmental organization. These larger organizations have a staff of internal auditors who work for the government. Internal auditors are concerned with the detection of fraud, and if requested, will perform a fraud audit. Internal auditing, unlike external auditing, is performed by an organization's own staff, and the direction of the audit can vary from determining compliance with management policy to fraud detection.

Good internal controls provide the strongest method for the prevention of NP fraud and theft. Yet, there are continual examples of fraudulent activities in NP organizations. The next section will review several of these methods.

A FEW OF THE USUAL SUSPECTS USED TO DEFRAUD

There are a number of methods that have been used to steal an NP's resources over the years. Today most NPs rely on electronic systems to record their accounting transactions. For that reason, most frauds involve unauthorized access to computer systems and the fraudulent manipulation of electronic records. For example, an employee may set up false employees in the electronic payroll records and collect the wage payments for those employees for their own use. Such frauds are easier to perpetuate with electronic records today than they would have been with paper documents in a previous era. A brief review of the traditional methods used to defraud organizations is briefly described next.

Lapping

When an NP organization is responsible for the collection of monies from its patrons, a lapping fraud can be implemented by the person responsible for collecting patron's checks. An NP organization may have one person responsible for several financial functions including the receiving of incoming checks, recording them in the books, and depositing the payments. The fraud begins when the clerk steals and cashes one of the patron's checks. The patron's account is not reduced by the amount of the incoming check. Before the patron or client has a chance to complain, the clerk receives another incoming check and credits the first account for the proper amount while still cashing other incoming checks for their own use. This results in a lapping of the payments from one account to another. Such a fraud requires the clerk to keep a "good" accounting of whose checks they are stealing; otherwise a patron might complain and instigate an investigation.

Fraudulent Purchases

If a single employee is responsible for purchasing goods, receiving them, journalizing entries in the accounting system, and writing checks for payment, it becomes relatively easy to purchase anything. In an NP with large fund flows, it could even be a car. In NPs with less funding, the fraudster would have to stick with large LCD screen TVs. In addition, a purchasing process with little internal control allows a purchasing agent to set up her own vendor, falsify the invoice, and bill the NP for goods that were never received.

Another version of this fraud is for the purchasing agent to work with a real vendor, falsify the invoice by overbilling, and then split the excess between themselves.

Payroll Fraud

If the internal controls are weak, it is possible for certain employees to report overtime hours that they have not really worked. For example, warehouse workers may have a practice of reporting overtime hours that have not been worked or that are worked whenever they need additional salary. In the latter case, the employees may stack items in an "overtime room" or have items stacked in such a manner that it requires extra time to load them for use. Such practices are likely condoned by the warehouse supervisor. Another version of payroll fraud includes the use of "ghost" workers. These are workers who appear on the payroll but who have left the organization and are not taken off the payroll schedule; or they are fictional workers who never were employees. Regardless of the method, they received payroll checks which are cashed by the payroll clerk for his own use.

Kiting

Check kiting may be considered to be a passé crime existing in the days when paper checks were used, but this is not true. Part of the reason for check kiting today is because banks are required to provide depositors with access to their cash deposits within a few days . . . even if the check has not cleared at a second bank.[1] Today's regulations require depository institutions to make deposited funds available according to specified time schedules. Depending on the nature of the deposit, the funds may be available to the customer on the next day. Anyone who has written a personal check on his account when the cash is not immediately in the account is playing the float and has taken the first step into check kiting.

Although kiting checks may seem to be an acceptable method to cover a budget deficit, it probably is not a good idea. Check kiting occurs due to the "float" time between when a check is written on a checking account in Bank One, for example, and deposited in Bank Two. It takes a few days for the check to go through the banking system and arrive at Bank One for collection.

There is no money in Bank One to cover a check written on the account in Bank One and deposited in Bank Two. The delay between the writing of a check and its arrival at Bank One for collection allows the check kiter to use Bank Two's money. To prevent Bank Two from discovering the fraud, the kiter deposits a check into her account in Bank Two from her account in Bank One. The kiter's objective is to keep checks floating back and forth between the banks so that neither bank will discover there is no money in either account. If successful, the scam will allow the check kiter to use the bank's money continuously over a long period of time by writing checks back and forth through Bank One and Bank Two. Depending on the nature of the scam, more than two banks can be involved.

Inventory Fraud

NPs need to prevent the theft of items in their inventories. NP inventories can include historical books or artifacts, medical supplies and equipment, furniture, vehicles, merchandise in gift stores, donated items, and easily removable electronic equipment. Obviously, inventories need to be physically secured so that no one can take valuable items out the door. Inventory fraud may be organized around the theft of "damaged" or fraudulently discounted goods. Collusion among ordering and receiving clerks allows employees to perpetuate such frauds. Employees take good inventory that they have reclassified as "damaged" and obtain cash for them in online auctions or garage sales. Other inventory frauds may be based on a fictitious sale and receivable to a phony buyer while the employee takes the inventory item home. Eventually the phony receivable on the sham sale is written off as uncollectible with no one the wiser.

Skimming Cash

Many NPs operate gift shops on their premises. There are libraries that sell their old books for a minimum value. The cash collected in such operations is a ready target for skimming. The skimming of cash occurs when an employee puts the cash in his pocket and does not record the sale. The sale may not be recorded in a cash register. Therefore, the sale is never entered into the accounting records. The cashier may decide that the best way to skim cash is to remove cash from the register and replace it with a fake check that later will be returned by the bank. In another scenario, the customer may receive a fake prenumbered receipt for the sale that is handwritten and thus the sale appears legitimate, but it is not. The same problem can occur with NP fund-raising events such as raffles, benefit dinners, and gaming nights. Many times, attendees do not expect to receive receipts when they attend these events so the cash receipts cannot be checked against the number of payments.

Shell Companies

Shell companies are fictitious businesses legally established and registered within a state to provide the appearance of a legitimate company. Such shell companies are set up by a fraudster who has authority to approve payments to be made. The fraudster uses the shell company to bill the NP for items such as consulting services. Consulting services are billed because it is difficult to prove that consulting services were not provided. The consulting invoices are approved by the NP manager who set up the shell company in the first place and who is providing the "consulting" services. Once the scheme is successful, it is possible to set up a number of other shell companies to keep all the fraudulent payments from only being paid to one fictitious company.

P-card Fraud

P-cards are credit cards given to the employees in an NP organization. The P-card allows NP employees to make purchases related to their legitimate activities without the need to encumber monies for each purchase and seek numerous spending authorizations. The difficulty with these cards is the temptation to charge personal purchases on the card. As the charges are not controlled, it is only through a later audit that the unauthorized charges are discovered. In those cases, the card holder may insist that there are outstanding credits that have not yet been charged to the card and

FUNNY BUSINESS

I feel lucky. William F. Blind and Vinita H. Sankey were found guilty of embezzling $150,000 of funds from the Cheyenne and Arapaho Tribes of Oklahoma. Blind and Sankey were on the Tribe's Business Committee and at various times served as officers on the Committee. Using their elected position, they overrode internal controls to submit fraudulent travel claims for conferences they did not attend, improper reimbursements for relatives' expenditures, purchased and cashed cashier's checks for personal use, purchased five vehicles, two riding lawnmowers, and a portable storage building. Along with Blind and Sankey, twelve other employees were sent to jail for participating in the embezzlement scheme.[2]

these charges will be taken off the card . . . shortly. In the meantime, the employee makes a rushed payment to refund the unauthorized personal charges. After a period of time passes, they can begin to make fraudulent charges on the card again.

The lack of NP personnel may mean an audit of expenditures would not be performed on any regular basis. In addition, the holder of a P-card may be a top executive at the NP organization. Consequently who is to determine that the charges on the P-card for what may appear to be unrelated to the NP's activities are truly illegitimate charges? The president of the University of the Cayman Islands, Hassan Syed, was dismissed for having more than $300,000 in unauthorized charges against his card. His whereabouts are currently unknown.[3]

Bid Rigging, Bribes, and the Other Usual Kickbacks

The rigging of bids on government and NP contracts can be performed in a number of ways, but it usually involves the payment of a kickback to the employee who was able to put together the deal. The bid is rigged when one bidder on the contract is provided with insider information that allows him to make a successful bid or when the "fix" is on who will receive the bid and the contract.

These are a few of the ways that fraud can be perpetuated in an NP, but the list could continue on into the use of forged documents to get loans, falsified vendors, the transfer of monies out of NP accounts and back into them before the auditors arrive, unauthorized use of NP equipment and labor on personal projects unrelated to the NP's official functions as well as other misappropriations of an NP's assets and resources.

DO I REALLY NEED TO READ ENGLISH TO DRIVE AN EIGHTEEN WHEELER?

My GPS speaks Russian. Mustafa Redzic operated the Bosna Truck Driving School in St. Louis, Missouri. Redzic was found guilty of conspiracy, wire fraud, mail fraud, and bribery. Redzic was bribing Troy Parr, who ran a state-approved commercial driver testing facility. Students had to pass the driving tests at the facility before they could receive their commercial truck driving license. In return for the payment of bribes from Redzic to Parr, Redzic's students were given favorable treatment on the driving exams. For example, they were given abbreviated easy exams or in some cases, they did not have to show up for the driving exams. It was estimated that Parr received bribes for giving out 469 commercial driver's licenses to Redzic's students.[4]

STOP MY CASH FROM DISAPPEARING . . . PLEASE

So you want to ensure your cash is not going into someone's pocket? OK, then you need to be certain the proper practices are used to secure your cash collections. For an NP, these cash flows may come from donations, sales at a gift store, library fines, sale of unwanted or used equipment or other assets, sale of donated assets, cash entrance fees to certain exhibits, and cash receipts from benefits and other similar events. As an example, consider the cash received from a benefit dinner put on by the NP to raise operating funds. Assume the dinner costs $20 per ticket and the money can be taken at the door or with a check in advance.

Figure 8.1 depicts the collection of cash at the door of the benefit event. In figure 8.1, three organizational units are involved in the collection of cash from the event. They are the person authorized to collect cash at the door, the Accounting Department, and in a small organization, the administrative staff. The Accounting Department is responsible for ensuring the transactions are properly recorded in the financial records. Administrative staff acts as an independent check on the cash deposited in the bank by performing a bank reconciliation to ensure all the collected cash was actually deposited. The preparation of the reconciliation needs to be separated from the cash collection function and the accounting staff who make the journal entries.

In the illustration when the cash is collected at the door, each person paying the $20 entrance charge receives a prenumbered ticket stub to enter the event. One portion of the ticket is kept by the person collecting the cash. Each person entering the door expects to receive a ticket stub to allow them to enter the event. Therefore, it would be difficult for the ticket issuer not give out a ticket and pocket the cash. The tickets are also prenumbered to allow a calculation to be made of how many tickets were issued. The stubs and the prenumbering both serve as an internal control against the loss of cash. Any missing or unaccounted numbers would have to be explained. Later, the number of tickets issued is checked against the cash balance in the collection box to ensure no cash has been removed from the collection box. As illustrated in figure 8.1, a deposit slip is made out by the ticket issuer for the cash balance in the collection box. Preparing the bank deposit immediately after counting the cash and separating this task from other cash functions reduces the risk of cash loss.

At such an event if there were no tickets issued, there is nothing to prevent the persons collecting cash at the door from slipping some of the twenty dollar bills in their pocket before they hand in the cash box and make out the deposit slip.

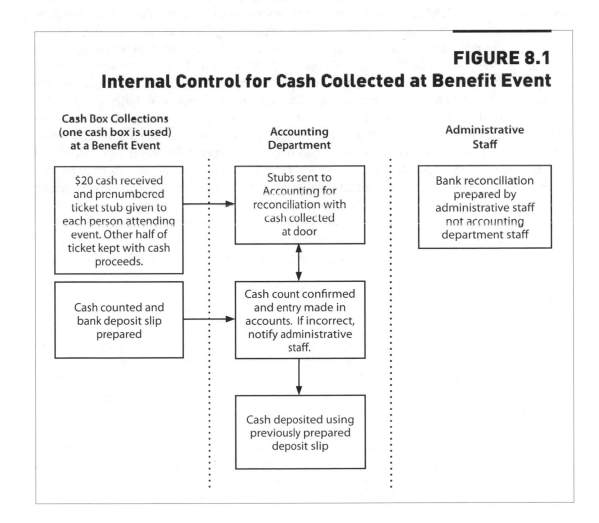

FIGURE 8.1

Internal Control for Cash Collected at Benefit Event

Cash Box Collections (one cash box is used) at a Benefit Event

Accounting Department

Administrative Staff

$20 cash received and prenumbered ticket stub given to each person attending event. Other half of ticket kept with cash proceeds.

Stubs sent to Accounting for reconciliation with cash collected at door

Bank reconciliation prepared by administrative staff not accounting department staff

Cash counted and bank deposit slip prepared

Cash count confirmed and entry made in accounts. If incorrect, notify administrative staff.

Cash deposited using previously prepared deposit slip

THE CASH SOLUTION

Where Is the Most Unsuspecting Place That I Can Find to Steal Cash?

I robbed the sheriff. Michel Holloran, an administrative assistant in the Jackson County Sheriff's Office, was responsible for processing funds from cash register receipts and other monies from the Sheriff's Traffic School and Victims' Impact Panel (for drunk drivers) programs. As a trusted employee, Michel counted the money in the cash register, made bank deposits, and managed the property control division. Another employee noticed an accounting discrepancy in the cash collections. An investigation was instituted. It was determined that Holloran was addicted to gambling. The investigation showed that there was little internal control over Michel's activities. The investigation uncovered a series of suspiciously voided checks in the records. In addition some of the cash register tapes were missing, meaning any amount of cash could have been deposited. Further, the cash remitted for deposit and the cash register collections were consistently different. The difference was the amount that Michel kept for her own personal use over the approximately three-year period that she conducted the scam. She also put checks back into the system from previously stolen deposits, a form of lapping. She was able to commit these frauds because her duties were not properly segregated. Michel was sentenced to 15 months in prison and required to pay $79,600.26 in restitution to Jackson County.[5]

The prenumbered ticket stubs, cash, and a bank deposit are sent to Accounting within twenty-four hours. The Accounting Department checks the cash against the number of tickets sold at the door. If there are no problems, the Accounting Department personnel use the previously prepared deposit slip and deposit the cash into the NP's bank. Accounting makes the entry in the NP's books for the cash collected. At the end of the month administrative staff prepares the bank reconciliation. It is important not to allow Accounting to make the reconciliation as they made the cash deposit. The separation of these two duties makes it difficult to conceal any cash that is not properly deposited as these two groups—Accounting and administrative staff—provide an independent verification that the deposit was correctly made.

In figure 8.1, the system for the collection of cash incorporates several aspects of good internal control. First, the collections are quickly checked against the tickets issued to patrons paying $20 at the door of the event and the transaction is quickly recorded in the accounting records. The act of collecting cash is segregated from recording the transaction in the NP's books. The bank reconciliation is prepared by the administrative staff to separate the cash depositing function from the reconciliation of the cash account. In order for a fraud to occur, there would have to be collusion among several individuals rather than just by one person.

WHO'S BUYING WHAT!

Beyond safeguarding the NP's assets, it is important to ensure that assets being purchased by the NP will not be taken home by employees. Even if assets are initially placed into use, there is no guarantee they will remain there as items such as computers and/or their projection systems, furniture, laptops, laser printers, and books can easily disappear. When assets are purchased, it is important to separate the job functions in the purchasing process to prevent the theft of these items.

Internal control practices should ensure that assets are only purchased when the proper authorizations are completed, their disposal is properly controlled, billings by vendors are correct (i.e., assets are actually ordered and ordered assets are received), and security practices are in effect. Typical forms and procedures used for good internal control include

---

LET'S AUTOMATE OUR SYSTEM

$998,000 and 38 Cents for Two Flat Washers!

Where is my million dollar cotter pin? A small parts supplier in the state of South Carolina charged the Department of Defense (DOD) $998,000 for shipping two washers to an Army base in Texas . . . and they got paid.

The DOD had automated their purchasing system with one flaw. If parts were shipped priority to a U.S. Army base or to combat areas (Iraq or Afghanistan), the shipping charges were paid without question. There was no oversight or internal control over priority shipping charges. DOD paid $455,009 to ship three machine screws costing $1.31 to Marines in Iraq, and $293,451 to ship an 89 cent off-the-shelf washer to Florida from South Carolina. Finally, a purchasing agent happened to notice a shipping charge for $969,000 for two additional washers and notified the DOD.

Two sisters, Corley and Darlene Wooten, who owned a parts supply company, had billed the DOD for over $20M in shipping costs over a six-year period. The sisters spent the money on houses, expensive cars, beach property, vacations, and jewelry. Corley Wooten is currently awaiting sentencing. Her sister committed suicide.[6]

---

asset request forms, new asset receipt forms, asset inventory control lists and bar-coded identification numbers, periodic physical checks to locate organizational assets, disposal forms, and lost asset reports.

The control practice over an NP's assets, whether they are donated or purchased, requires the segregation of duties involved in the acquisition process. Figure 8.2 highlights these purchase control practices. In figure 8.2, the Purchasing, Accounting, and Receiving Departments are shown. The Purchasing Department receives and reviews numbered fixed asset purchase request forms from those organizational units that are asking for new assets. The NP in Figure 8.2 uses an electronic format for asset acquisition, and any printed hard copies are used for filing information outside the ordering system itself. The fixed asset request form exists as a screen document, and it provides information about the need for the asset, the suggested vendor, a description of the old asset to be replaced if there is one, details as to how acquisition will affect budgeted amounts, and how it provides value to the department's mission goal. Depending on the cost of the asset and whether it is part of approved budget expenditures, the request form may need to be authorized by the department head, the director of the NP, and the board.

Figure 8.2 illustrates the ordering process as it moves through the Purchasing, Accounting, and Receiving Departments. The approved request form is sent to Accounting. Accounting prepares the purchase order and encumbers the funds for the purchase price. With the preparation of the purchase order and fund encumbrance recorded, the transaction is in the accounting system. A copy of the purchase order is electronically sent to the vendor. The Receiving Department will check the screen copies of the purchase order with the invoice when the items are delivered into Receiving by the vendor. Having the request for a new asset verified in the Purchasing Department and the purchase order and fund encumbrance recorded into the system by the Accounting Department segregates these functions and provides for better control over the acquisition of assets.

The new asset should not be sent directly to the Purchasing Department or to Accounting. Instead the Receiving Department checks all received items to ensure they are undamaged, the correct quantity of items were received, items are charged on the vendor's invoice at the correct amount, and, of course, that they were actually ordered by the NP. The receiving

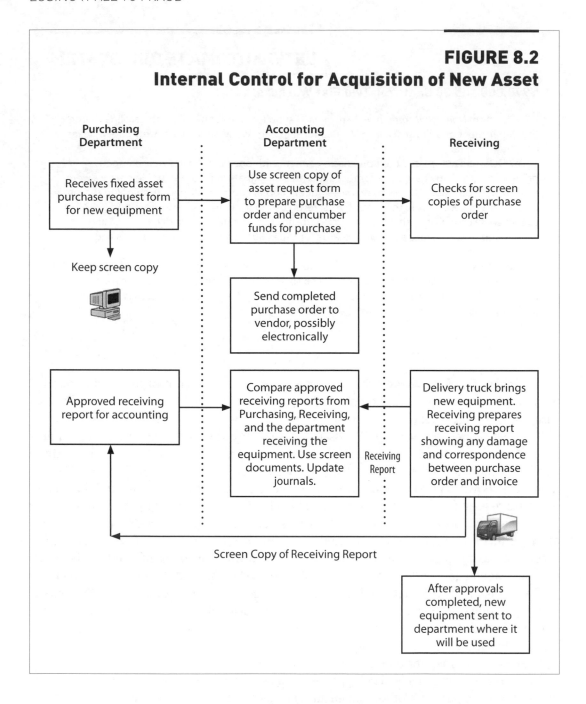

FIGURE 8.2
Internal Control for Acquisition of New Asset

department prepares an electronic receiving report that verifies the order. This receiving report is compared by the Purchasing Department with the purchase order. Accounting checks all documents. The use of a separate Receiving Department helps to reduce theft risk because it segregates the ordering function from the receiving function. When these functions cannot be separated from each other, the risk of asset loss is increased.

In a small NP, it is difficult to separate these three functions from each other. Accounting, for example, may prepare the purchase order, record all entries, and check the asset when it is received. It should be obvious that when one individual is responsible for ordering, recording transactions, and receiving assets, the risk of fraud and theft is much higher.

The final step in the purchasing process is to send the asset to the department that ordered the item. After all checks are made between Purchasing, Accounting and Receiving, the asset is sent to the department that ordered the item. The department ordering the asset signs the receiving report indicating it accepts the new asset. In Accounting, an approved receiving report is checked against the purchase order, the receiving report, and the invoice. If everything is in order, journal entries are made to record the new asset in the NP's books.

The new asset is assigned an inventory number by the Accounting Department. Inventory control lists should be maintained in the Accounting Department and not in the department where the asset is housed. The inventory number identification number contained on a bar code should be affixed to the asset in a manner so that it cannot easily be removed. Periodically the NP's inventory should be checked against inventory control lists to determine if any assets have been lost or removed from the facility.

DISPOSING OF ASSETS

Even if the practice of purchasing new assets follows good internal control procedures, assets can still be misappropriated if their disposal practices are weakly controlled. New assets may be switched along with their inventory tags with old assets. When the "old" asset is taken out of service, it is really the new asset, and the employee takes it home.

The disposal of any asset with a significant purchase price should be initiated by the department where the asset is being used. A request for disposal should be prepared by the department where the asset is housed and list the reason for the disposal along with the asset inventory identification number. The request form should include sign-off authorizations from the department head, director, and, if necessary, the board. The approved request will go to Accounting. Accounting personnel will check inventory records and confirm the whereabouts of the asset. For good internal control to exist, the asset's inventory tag should be checked to ensure it has not been removed or switched. If cash is received for the old asset, internal control procedures for the receipt of cash need to be in effect to ensure the cash is properly collected and recorded in the accounts.

SUMMARY

Managerial responsibility includes making sure the NP is operating in an efficient and effective manner, but it also extends to safeguarding the NP's assets. It is a particularly hard setback for an organization that has succeeded in correcting a budget deficit to discover that its operations need to be further curtailed due to the theft of its cash or other assets.

The root of fraudulent behavior does not usually start with the idea, "I think I will steal millions and that's why I took this job." Fraudulent behavior starts a little at a time. If you can "tweak" or "finesse" the numbers a little and no one notices, the next time it can probably be done a little more without any negative consequences. The organizational attitude toward financial shortcuts and ethical behavior come from the top NP managers. If there is an attitude of trying to get "off the hook," then the underlying moral tone in the organization needs to be questioned. When the top executives in an NP organization along with a substantial number of other employees who participated in a fraud are all sentenced, there is a deep underlying ethical problem existing in that organization. Fraudulent activities start with small unethical steps that can eventually cross the line to illegal behavior without much additional thought.

NOTES

1. See UCC Article 4 and Regulation CC (12 CFR 229). Regulation CC (12 CFR 229) implements two laws—the Expedited Funds Availability Act (EFA Act), which was enacted in August 1987 and became effective in September 1988, and the Check Clearing for the 21st Century Act (Check 21), which was passed in October 2003 and became effective on October 28, 2004.

2. "Two Former Elected Cheyenne-Arapaho Tribal Officials Convicted of Conspiracy and Embezzlement from the Tribe," *Crime Reporter USA,* February 9, 2010, www.crimereporterusa.com.

3. See Basia Pioro, "The Saga of Hassan Syed," *Caymanian Compass,* December 29, 2008, www.caycompass.com/cgi-bin/CFPnews.cgi?ID=1036343.

4. "Truck Driving School Owner Sentenced on Bribery and Fraud Charges," Department of Justice Press Release, June 16, 2008, http://stlouis.fbi.gov/dojpressrel/pressrel08/sl061608.htm.

5. "Former County Employee Pleads Guilty," Department of Justice Press Release, October 11, 2006, www.justice.gov/usao/or/PressReleases/20061011_Sheriff_Employee.htm.

6. "Lexington Woman Pleads Guilty," Department of Justice Press Release, August 16, 2007, www.justice.gov/criminal/npftf/pr/press . . . /aug/08-16-07ccorley-plea.pdf.

NINE

DIVING INTO A FINANCIAL HOLE: PART I

I've worked out my monthly fixed cost figure which is £160.95.
But how do I do the VC per UNIT. It's SO confusing.

Unknown

I'd rather play golf and break even, than work hard and come out ahead.

Mike Donald

Usually the term "break-even" is used whenever an NP manager is hoping that revenues will cover organizational costs during an annual financial period. Yet, break-even concerns must begin at a more micro-level than annually for an entire organization. For example when an NP "believes" it can raise funds through a benefit dinner, raffling of an HD TV, or the selling of T-shirts, it is useful to know how many tickets or T-shirts must be sold for the NP to cover its costs. Without that information, the NP could be diving into a financial hole. Such small financial mistakes eventually lead the entire organization into a financial sinkhole.

In planning a fund-raising event, there must be enough ticket sales to cover the NP's costs of purchasing meals, the giveaway HD TV, and other items. In this case, break-even analysis allows managers to determine how much revenue is needed to cover costs as well as any excess funding collected at the event. Organizational resources are limited, and it is important to use them in the most productive manner possible. Methods such as break-even analysis help curtail seat-of-the-pants decision making as a justification for resource use.

BREAK-EVEN 101

A useful managerial technique for making short-term operating decisions is break-even analysis. Break-even analysis utilizes projections of costs, revenues, contributions, and appropriations to determine when total costs are equal to total revenues (contributions and appropriations). The point of intersection between total cost and total revenue is called the break-even point because there is no profit. Operations conducted below the break-even point result in losses or reduction in resources; operations above the break-even point represent a profit or inflow of NP resources. NP operations can only operate below the break-even point for a limited time before the viability of the organization is called into question.

Break-even analysis can be used for a number of different purposes in NPs. For example, if a new self-sustaining service is going to be provided by the NP, break-even analysis can be used to determine the number of patrons required to use the service at the break-even point—the point where total costs and total fees are equal. Break-even analysis is useful in identifying those fixed costs or variable costs that can be lowered in order to break-even. When budget cuts are necessary, break-even analysis will help managers determine which of their self-sustaining units cannot cover their operating costs. If an NP is operating a coffee service or gift shop, selling T-shirts, book bags, or posters, break-even analysis is useful in determining how many units have to be sold before profits are earned. The analysis determines if the project is financially feasible without going into a financial hole.

Determining the break-even point is a relatively simple calculation. Two versions of the equation used to calculate the break-even point are shown in figure 9.1.

The denominator in equation 2 in figure 9.1 is called the contribution margin. The contribution margin is defined as the difference between the per-unit selling price of an item and its variable cost per unit, and that relationship is shown in the denominator in equation 1. The contribution margin contributes to reducing fixed costs or above break-even, the earning of profits. To calculate the break-even point, costs must be separated into fixed and variable costs. The fixed costs represent the numerator of the equation, and the variable costs are used in calculating the contribution margin.

As an example, assume an NP is considering selling book bags.

FIGURE 9.1
Two Equations Used to Calculate the Break-even Point

$$(1)\ \text{Break-even point} = \frac{\text{Fixed cost dollars}}{\underset{\text{(per unit)}}{\text{Selling price}} - \underset{\text{(per unit)}}{\text{Variable cost}}}$$

$$(2)\ \text{Break-even point} = \frac{\text{Fixed cost dollars}}{\text{Contribution margin per unit}}$$

The fixed cost of the book bags is their purchased cost from the supplier, which in this case is $12. A total of 300 bags will be purchased, none of which can be returned to the supplier. The NP intends to sell them for $15 each. The question to ask is, how many bags will have to be sold to break even?

The computation of the break-even point requires that the contribution margin be determined. The contribution margin is equal to the difference between the selling price and the variable costs. As there are no variable costs, the contribution margin is equal to the selling price of $15. The break-even point is determined as follows:

$$\text{Break-even point in units} = \frac{\textit{Total fixed costs ($12 x 300)}}{\text{Contribution margin ($15)}} = 240 \text{ bags}$$

In this example, the NP must sell 240 book bags before it starts receiving any profits above the original cost for the book bags of $3,600 ($12 x 300). If the NP should sell all 300 book bags, it will earn a profit of $900 ($15 received for a book bag x 60 book bags sold above the break-even point of 240 (or $3 x 300). If the NP does not believe that 240 book bags can be sold, it should reduce the order. In this example, the break-even point is equal to 80 percent of the number of book bags they order (12/15 = 80 percent).

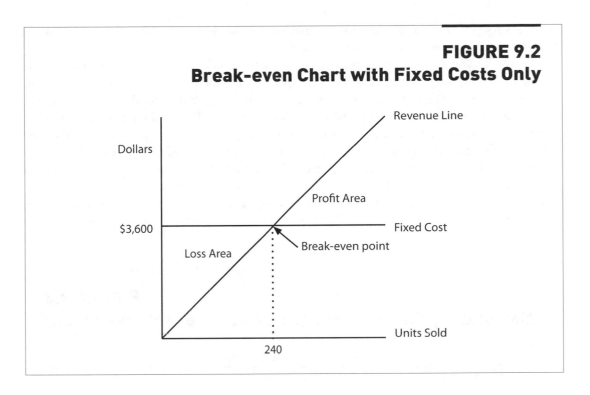

FIGURE 9.2
Break-even Chart with Fixed Costs Only

This calculation provides a quick, easy method to determine if a simple fund-raising event will result in net inflows of cash to the NP. Remember that this is a fund-raising event based on managerial estimates, and these estimates can be overly optimistic.

Figure 9.2 presents a graphic illustration of the break-even point of the book bag fund-raising event.

In figure 9.2, the break-even point is shown in both dollars and units. The horizontal line on the graph represents the fixed costs of $3,600, and the break-even point occurs along this line where it is intersected by revenues. There are no variable costs. The number of book bags sold at the break-even point is 240 bags, and it is illustrated with a dotted line from the horizontal axis to the break-even point. The profit and loss areas are shown above and below the break-even point, respectively. When variable costs are included in the break-even cost mix, the analysis is noticeably changed.

To incorporate variable costs into a break-even problem, assume that the book bags will be personalized with the patron's name when the bag is purchased. The artist, Mr. Z., who will do the personalization, requires a fixed payment of $300, and his contract requires that a rate of $0.50 per letter must be paid by the NP to him. The NP wants to maintain a break-even point of 240 bags as previously determined. If the average name has a total of ten letters, the break-even point of 240 book bags will require a total of 2,400 letters. What should the NP charge patrons per letter on the book bags?

The selling price and the cost of the bags purchased remain the same, so the break-even point is still 240 bags or 2,400 letters. In this illustration, a price that patrons are charged per letter must be determined at an already specified break-even point. The easiest method for solving this problem is to place all the information into the break-even equation (equation 1 in figure 9.1).

The break-even equation is used to make the calculation in figure 9.3. In the equation, the unknown selling price and the variable cost of $0.50 for each letter are in the denominator. The fixed cost of $300 is the numerator. When the equation is solved for the unknown selling price, it is equal to $0.625. This is the minimum price the NP should charge for each letter placed on a personalized bag. The average patron's name of ten letters can be placed on the bag for a minimum charge of $6.25 ($0.625 x 10). As this is a fund raiser for the NP, a price higher than the minimum per letter price of $0.625 should be charged. If the NP charges a price of $1 per letter, they will make $0.375 for each letter put on a bag.

Figure 9.4 shows the break-even analysis for the monogrammed letters only, in a graphic break-even format. This graph is similar to the one shown in figure 9.2; however, it includes

---

FIGURE 9.3

Calculating the Price per Letter at the Break-even Point

$$\text{Break-even point (2,400 letters)} = \frac{\text{Fixed cost dollars (\$300)}}{\text{Unknown selling price (X)} - \text{Variable cost (\$0.50)}}$$

$$2{,}400 \text{ letters} = \frac{\$300}{\text{Unknown selling price (X)} - \$0.50}$$

$$\text{Unknown selling price (X)} = \$0.625$$

FIGURE 9.4

Break-even Chart with Variable and Fixed Costs for Personalized Letters

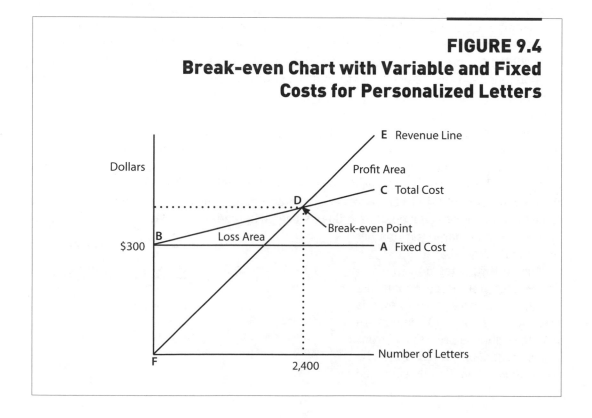

a variable cost component. The fixed cost is the fixed payment of $300 required to be paid to Mr. Z. The break-even point is shown in the number of letters (2,400) and dollars ($1,500 = $0.625 x 2,400) charged patrons at the break-even point. This graph is different from the one shown in Figure 9.2 because the variable costs are included as a triangle (ABC) above fixed costs. The areas of profit (D, E, C) and loss (D, B, F) are shown above and below, respectively, the break-even point on the chart.

Another break-even application is to determine the level of fixed costs that can be incurred before a loss is experienced by the NP. Assume an NP wants to install a coffee kiosk and have it run by one part-time employee. The NP director wants to know the weekly revenue from the kiosk and whether it will cover the cost of leasing the coffee/latte machine. Most of the cost and revenue projections will need to be estimated. The lease payments are a fixed charge. The rest of the information about the proposed operation follows:

COFFEE OR NOT?

Part-time worker: $12 per hour working 22 hours per week five days a week with no benefits provided

Coffee: $27 per bag; each bag makes 200 cups of coffee

Milk: $3 per half gallon; ½ gallon makes 100 cups of coffee

Utilities (water, electricity, etc.): Charged out at $2 per hour that the kiosk is open

Average price for cup sold: $4

Average daily cups sold: 60 cups

Monthly rent on coffee equipment: $550

THE CALCULATION

Step 1: Separate Variable and Fixed Costs

Fixed: Weekly Equipment Rent	$137.50
Variable: Weekly Salary	$264
Weekly Coffee Cost: (300 cups per week or 1 ½ bags)	$40.50
Weekly Milk Cost: (300 cups per week or 1½ gallons)	$9
Utilities: ($2 x 22 hours per week)	$44

Step 2: Determine the Revenue

Weekly Revenue: (300 cups x $4)	$1,200

Step 3: Determine the Weekly Profit = $705

Weekly Profit: ($1,200—$137.50—$264—$40.50—$9—$44) = $703.50

The director reviewed the computation. Although the projections showed a $705 weekly profit, the results were based on a lot of estimates. After reviewing the computation, the director asked, "What is the minimum number of cups that need to be sold for a zero profit?" If the weekly profit were zero, the sales revenue would drop by $705 to $495 or 124 cups per week ($495/$4). The profit would be zero and the revenue would drop from $703.50 to $496.50 or ($496.50/4) or around 124 cups per week. At this rate, a minimum of 25 cups would have to be sold daily. If this goal cannot be exceeded, the project should not be started.

Break-even analysis has numerous applications. But before several of those applications are described, some of the limitations in break-even analysis should be taken into account.

BREAK-EVEN LIMITATIONS

There are several limitations that need to be considered when break-even analysis is applied. The first limitation is related to the requirement to separate fixed and variable costs. Separating fixed and variable costs may be difficult. First, some costs may be a mixture of both fixed and variable costs, but they still need to be separated into their fixed and variable components. Placing all costs into a fixed or variable category is somewhat arbitrary, and unless this is considered, incorrect decisions could result.

Another limitation is related to the concept of fixed costs and the time period under analysis. Break-even decisions are based on a short-term time period. In the short-term period, costs will maintain their fixed/variable relationship. But fixed costs may change in the long term. The time period of the analysis needs to be carefully considered when decisions are based on the break-even point.

As an example of this difficulty, consider a break-even decision related to the patron fee charged for searching a proprietary database. Assume that the Reference Department currently accesses only one database and has isolated the costs related to its database search functions: $350 per year for depreciation of equipment (terminal, furniture, etc.), a $150 fee for a maintenance agreement, a minimum $100 charge for access to the database, and $1,200 for yearly training updates. There is a $15 per-hour charge for the staff person conducting the search, a $30 hourly charge by the vendor, and a $10 communication charge per hour. The library wants to determine the break-even charge per search, assuming that 500 searches will be conducted per year. The average search takes a half hour. Using the break-even equation, these costs can be separated into fixed and variable components.

The fixed costs are depreciation ($350), maintenance charges ($150), minimum service charge ($100), and training ($1,200) and equals $1,800. The per-hour charges are variable costs. The break-even equation incorporates these costs to solve for the unknown charge per search as shown in figure 9.5.

FIGURE 9.5
**Calculating the Charge per Search
at the Break-even Point**

$$\text{Break-even searches (500)} = \frac{\text{Fixed costs (\$1,800)}}{\text{Cost charged per search (X)} - \text{Variable costs (\$27.50)*}}$$

Cost charged per search (X) = $31.10 or $32 or $16 per half-hour search

* The hourly rate for searches is $55 per hour ($15 + $30 + $10) or $27.50 per half hour.

In solving the equation, the result is a break-even charge of $32 per search when 500 searches are made. This is the average charge for searches. In reviewing the equation relationships, it appears that the best way to reduce the average cost per search would be to increase the number of searches performed each year. This conclusion is reached because the total fixed costs are assumed to be constant, and variable costs will remain constant per unit. If all fixed costs remain constant, this conclusion is true.

Using the break-even equation, it can be determined that the average hourly cost per search will be lowered to $29.30 if the number of searches is doubled to 1,000. Assume that the library decides to promote this service and increase the number of searches as a convenience to its patrons and to lower the hourly fee charged to patrons. The analysis assumes that fixed costs remain constant. But, will they stay constant?

To perform 1,000 searches, the number of proprietary databases is increased to serve a wider variety of search requests. When this occurs, the service costs increase. With an expansion in databases, additional staff training is necessary. Even if the number of database searches were not increased, training costs would increase in order to qualify more staff needed to perform the expanded number of searches. As the number of searches is expanded, there is a higher usage of equipment. Charges for usage, such as depreciation, would increase to reflect additional usage. All these costs are fixed costs, and although they are fixed in the short run, they are not fixed in the long run.

The time horizon for many managerial decisions extends beyond the short term used in break-even analysis. In this example, the increase in fixed costs causes the average cost per search to remain higher than anticipated. It is important to remember that decisions structured around a short-term time frame may lead to unanticipated mistakes. Care needs to be exercised in using any decision-making tool.

Two other limitations of break-even analysis should be mentioned: the linearity assumption and the effect of the relevant range issues. The linearity assumption states that the changing relationship between volume and costs is linear—a straight line. Some costs do not follow the linearity assumption, such as costs that step up in constant increments. An example of a step cost is the fixed cost of hiring a staff supervisor. This fixed salary cost steps up with each new supervisor hired; it is not linear. Also, not all costs maintain the same linear relationship with volume over the entire volume range. Additionally, variable costs may not increase at the same constant dollar amount per unit over the entire range of the break-even chart. Some costs may have a curvilinear relationship to volume. Therefore, care needs to be exercised so that the linearity assumption will not mislead decision makers.

A final limitation of break-even analysis is related to the relevant range. The relevant range is the high and low volume areas within which the NP typically operates. Outside the relevant range, cost behavior cannot be predicted. In the break-even charts shown in the chapter, the cost and revenue lines are drawn from zero to very high volume levels. As the NP has never operated in these extremely low or high volume levels, it cannot be predicted

WHERE HAVE THEY ALL GONE?

At Community Connections, the demand for such services increased so much in 2009 that "we thought there was no way we were even going to break even," Frazier said. They did. Experts say this year could be worse as the sector's three main revenue sources—charitable donations, government funding and fee for service—falter.

"I think it's a real threat," said Rena Coughlin, chief executive of the Nonprofit Center of Northeast Florida. Nationally, she said, forecasters say that as many as 100,000 nonprofits will be gone by the end of the recession.[2]

how costs will behave in these areas. Costs and revenues are likely to behave as shown in the break-even charts only within the relevant range which are the volume levels at which the organization typically conducts its business operations.

BREAK-EVEN ANALYSIS AND APPROPRIATIONS

In nonprofit organizations, break-even analysis can be applied to situations where there are no revenues. Instead of earning revenues, the NP receives appropriations. The next examples of decision making use budget appropriations combined with break-even analysis. When a budget appropriation is considered, it means that fixed costs are reduced by the appropriation. Essentially, a budget appropriation is deducted from the total fixed costs, and the remainder is used as the numerator of the break-even equation. Afterwards, the calculations are performed as previously illustrated.

For example, assume that a public health service is starting a shut-in service. The cost components of this service will include an assignment of staff time, a public relations campaign to advertise the service, training costs of staff, additional supplies, additional use of telephones, and new equipment such as fax machines, audiovisual equipment, and a van. The costs can be separated into yearly fixed costs of $75,000 and variable costs of $18 per shut-in. Assume that the health agency has received a state grant of $25,000. Because the grant does not cover the NP's cost of providing the service, a service fee must be charged. The number of clients using the service will determine the NP's total variable costs for the service. It is estimated the number of clients using the service in the first year will be 1,000 shut-ins. The agency would like to know the fee they should charge.

The first step to finding the answer is to subtract the grant of $25,000 from the fixed costs of operating the program, $75,000. The net fixed costs of $50,000 and the variable cost per shut-in are placed into the break-even equation in figure 9.6 to determine the fee to charge. In this case, the $68 fee is more than the per-unit variable cost because the fee must recover the fixed costs of $50,000 not covered by the state grant. A break-even chart for an NP receiving an appropriation is similar to the ones shown earlier in the chapter with the exception of a $50,000 appropriation line drawn straight across the bottom of the chart below the total fixed cost line.

If the assumptions are changed so the grant specifies that a maximum of $5 can be charged per shut-in by any health agency accepting the grant, the number of clients wanting services will expand. Assume the grant now provides an appropriation of $88,000 or $13,000 above the NP's fixed costs of $75,000. The granting agency increased the funding from $25,000 to $88,000 to entice the health agency to accept the grant. The finance officer at the granting

---

FIGURE 9.6
Break-even Analysis with an Appropriation

$$\text{Break-even (1,000 shut-ins)} = \frac{\text{Remaining fixed costs (\$50,000)}}{\text{Fee (X) –Variable cost (\$18)}}$$

$$\text{Shut-ins 1,000} = \frac{\$50,000}{X - \$18}$$

$$\text{Fee (X)} = \$68 \text{ Yearly fee}$$

agency prepared the following break-even analysis for the health agency. The finance office shows the director of the health agency that the break-even point is still 1,000 shut-ins.

Break-even (X) = *$13,000 grant proceeds above fixed costs*

$5 service fee—$18 variable costs = 1,000 shut-ins

The director of the health agency believes that when the service fee is $5 the number of shut-ins wanting the service will expand to 1,800 not 1,000. What financial situation will the NP be facing if the grant is accepted? Again, the break-even equation can help in making this determination.

If 1,800 shut-ins are expected to request the service when the fee is dropped to $5 should the NP accept the $88,000 grant? The break-even chart in figure 9.7 is used to help make the determination. In figure 9.7, it can be seen that the break-even point with services provided to 1,000 clients ($5 service fee and $88,000 grant) is $93,000. When services are provided to more than 1,000 clients, the NP begins to incur a deficit in the program.

At the bottom of figure 9.7, the computation is shown for 1,800 shut-ins enrolled in the program. At that service level, a deficit of $10,400 will occur. This is the distance between Point A and Point B in figure 9.7. The deficit increases as the number of shut-ins increases.

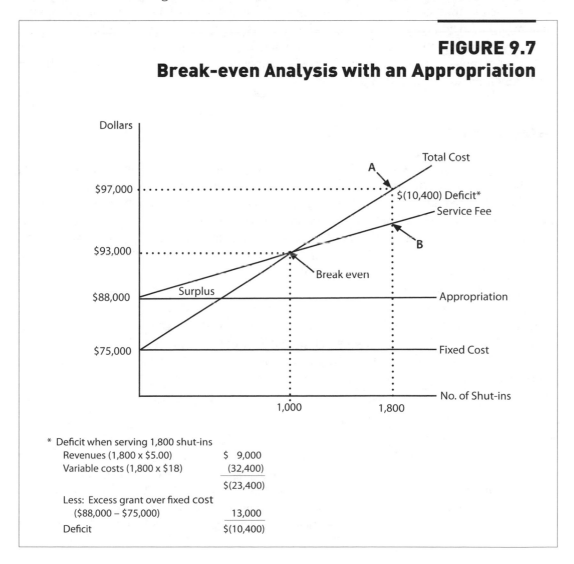

FIGURE 9.7
Break-even Analysis with an Appropriation

* Deficit when serving 1,800 shut-ins

Revenues (1,800 x $5.00)	$ 9,000
Variable costs (1,800 x $18)	(32,400)
	$(23,400)
Less: Excess grant over fixed cost	
($88,000 – $75,000)	13,000
Deficit	$(10,400)

This trend is shown in the break-even chart where the loss above 1,800 shut-ins continues to widen or increase.[3] The deficit spending required by an NP accepting such a grant may not be readily apparent, but any NP that does accept grants of this nature must be ready to supplement the funds provided by the granting agency.

A similar deficit can also occur when a funding agency provides initial start-up funds but then requires the NP accepting the funding to continue the program in the future with their own resources. Other grants may be so time consuming and require such costly paperwork and follow-ups that the tracing of all costs to them results in an NP deficit on the grant.

It should be noted in figure 9.7 that as service levels fall below the break-even point the health agency recognizes a surplus from the shut-in program. This is a reversal of the typical break-even analysis shown in a for-profit organization. Consequently, managers may question how aggressively they should promote the program, whether the NP will be able to handle the widening deficit if the program expands to more shut-ins above the break-even point, or if a result of running the program will mean budgetary curtailment in other areas. As shown in figure 9.7, decreasing the number of shut-ins serviced below the break-even point increases the surplus from this program. Usually any surplus would be returned to the granting agency, but such action prevents the NP from incurring a deficit that it cannot support.

For a program that charges no fee and has no appropriation, the deficit or loss begins as soon as the program starts. The shut-in program is an example of a service that is receiving an appropriation and charges a fee that is less than its variable costs. As a result, this program is simply delaying the initial onset of the inevitable deficit. The point of these illustrations is that no standard assumptions about cost relationships should be accepted until all cost behaviors are examined and understood.

SUMMARY

In order for NPs to break-even, they need to ensure that each operation they undertake is itself breaking even. An NP that is not breaking even on its business operations has a limited period in which it can exist before the organization needs to shut its doors. It is necessary to study each minor project, grant, or extension of services to determine if there is a chance for such activities to break-even. When the organization's annual financial reports are viewed from a break-even perspective, it is usually too late to make any corrective changes because the financial results for the year are complete.

When break-even analysis is used in the proper format, it can be used to project financial estimates into the future. The analysis may mean the NP has to turn down funding "opportunities" in order for the organization to remain a viable organization. Only with well structured financial decision making can an NP help the most people.

The next chapter will explain how NPs dive into a financial hole when making long-term decisions.

NOTES

1. Stephanie Strom, "Nonprofit Groups Foresee Tough Year," *New York Times*, March 21, 2010, www.nytimes.com/2010/03/22/us/22charity.html.

2. Deirdre Conner, "Nonprofits Sustainability Depends on Innovation," March 1, 2010, http://jacksonville.com/news/metro/2010-03-01/story/nonprofits_sustainability_depends_on_innovation.

3. In figure 9.7, $93,000 is equal to the appropriation of $88,000 plus the $5,000 received in service fees ($5 x 1,000 clients). The $97,000 is calculated in the same manner as the appropriation of $88,000 plus the $5 service fee times the 1,800 clients.

TEN

DIVING INTO A FINANCIAL HOLE: PART II

The most unfair thing about life is the way it ends. I mean, life is tough. It takes up a lot of your time. What do you get at the end of it? A Death! What's that, a bonus? I think the life cycle is all backwards.

George Carlin

Chapter 10 begins the explanation of a technique that is needed in any NP manager's financial toolbox as they make long-term purchase decisions. Without applying the financial analysis in the chapter, a manager is likely to push their NP into a long-term financial sinkhole. Recovering from a poor break-even decision is possible, but recovering from incorrect long-term financial decisions can take years . . . if ever. Unless the NP organization receives additional donor or agency funding to make up for these financial mistakes, the ability of the NP to provide services to the public will have to be curtailed.

The managerial technique that allows an NP manager to evaluate long-term purchase decisions and stay out of a financial hole is called life-cycle costing (LCC). LCC is defined as the accumulation of all costs related to an asset, project, service, or management policy over its entire life from start to completion or abandonment. In some organizations, no long-term purchase decisions can be completed without an LCC analysis showing the best and next-best purchase choices and reasons for a final selection. LCC analysis goes beyond reviewing the purchase price of an asset or the initial cost of providing a new service. With LCC, the annual operating costs of an asset in addition to the asset's initial purchase price need to be evaluated. Operating costs include the costs of support, maintenance and repair, personnel training, debugging systems, and equipment overhauling or upgrading costs. Depending on the asset, the after-purchase costs can be equal to 100 times the initial cost of the asset. If decisions are made to acquire assets based solely on a comparison of purchase prices with budget appropriations, decisions are being made without considering the NP's long-term viability.

For example, assume that an NP organization needs a printer for making color copies. The organization is trying to decide between two printers. One choice is a laser printer that costs $489. The other choice is an ink jet printer that costs $89. Both printers come with starter ink cartridges or packs. The manager can save $400 by buying the ink jet printer. It seems to be a logical decision to buy the ink jet printer, but the reason the ink jet printer is so inexpensive is because the manufacturers expect to recoup their costs and make a profit by continuing to sell ink jet packs to the purchasers of their printer. It is estimated that the cost of ink for an ink jet printer is about $10,000 per gallon. A manager just dove into a long-term financial hole as the NP continues to service the ink jet printer over its life cycle. These decisions transfer limited organizational resources into overhead costs and away from value-added funding for NP patrons.

A COUPLE OF CAVEATS

The use of LCC analysis with long-term projects requires the application of time value of money concepts.[1] In the examples presented in this chapter, time value of money concepts is not used. Examples of LCC and present value analyses can be found in G. Stevenson Smith's *Managerial Accounting for Libraries and Other Not-for-Profit Organizations*. Another caveat is that LCC is not related to the calculation of net income. With LCC, cash flow is the primary concern, not profit or loss. As a result, the NP's accounting system cannot easily provide information about the projected LCC. Such cost estimates have to be provided by managers.[2]

When assets have a very short life, it is not necessary to use LCC analysis as the comparisons made with LCC are commonsense applications. LCC also loses its practical utility as the life of an asset's life begins to extend further and further beyond five years because projections become subject to larger estimation error. Another consideration regarding estimations is that they may be purposely biased by managers to provide a more favorable result in asset acquisition tradeoffs. Thus, these estimates need to be scrutinized both before and after making a purchase to ensure that realistic estimates were used.

LCC determines the total cost of the purchased asset over its entire life. In that process, LCC analysis also incorporates any cost reductions or cash inflows related to an asset. There are several reasons why an asset may experience cash inflows. For example, if it is estimated that an asset can be sold for salvage at the end of its useful life, the salvage dollars are a cash inflow. Salvage values are estimates that can change if the asset's useful life is over- or underestimated or if premature obsolescence of the asset occurs. But, salvage values reduce the cost of the asset and provide the NP with a positive cash inflow at the end of an asset's life. In addition, cash inflows from an asset can come from the generation of revenues. A photocopy machine and photocopy revenues are an example of such cash inflows.

Finally, nonquantifiable factors, such as the quality of vendor services and political realities in the NP, are likely to be just as important as financial information in the asset selection process. These nonquantifiable factors need to be considered as asset recommendations are made.

LET'S TALK LCC

The NP's cost commitment to an asset grows after a purchase is made. This cost growth occurs as annual operating costs are incurred. Operating costs can be significantly different among assets that are designed to provide the same service. For example, an NP analyzing the purchase choices between web servers may determine that a savings in energy costs per machine per year would occur if a more expensive but faster working model were purchased. The faster working server uses less electricity and requires less maintenance. In this case, an analysis of future operating costs significantly affects a purchase decision.

The operating costs of an asset are preset in the design of the equipment. This preset cost is determined by the performance criteria for speed and other selected options. For example, the stress levels in a building designed to be a library are higher than those of similar-sized office buildings. The design requirements for increased structural support in a library increase the building's cost. This cost increase was preset in the planning stages of the new building. Without those higher construction costs, expenditures would be transferred to the building's annual repair and maintenance operating costs.

If a new photocopying machine is to be purchased and the primary performance criterion for selection is the fastest speed for making copies, then that particular requirement will be the cost driver—cause of cost incurrence—that forces up the purchase price of a machine. The increase in the purchase price was built into the design or planning stage by the performance requirement for copy speed.

DUSTY ROADS? MAYBE NOT

The Asphalt Pavement Alliance (APA) has released new software for life-cycle cost analysis (LCCA) of pavements. The new software, called LCCAExpress, uses the principles recommended by the Federal Highway Administration (FHWA) to compare the economics of alternative designs for a given road project.[3]

The annual operating costs of new assets have the capacity to consume larger and larger portions of future budget appropriations due to initial design choices. Without LCC analysis, the organization approaches its future in a hit-or-miss fashion and has the potential to dive into a financial hole without even knowing it.

PROJECTING LIFE-CYCLE COSTS

When projecting LCC, consider the cost of a cruise ship vacation. In planning a cruise, the vacationer looks at the purchase price of the ticket for a two-week cruise that includes meals and says, "Great!" Yet, it would only be a naïve vacationer who expected the ticket cost to be the entire cost of the cruise. Travel costs have to be added to get to and from the departure port. At least, 20 percent of the ticket price needs to be added for tips. More needs to be added for optional activities and port activities. Then there are taxes and port departure fees. So the added costs beyond the ticket price of the cruise may put the vacationer in debt. A similar situation faces NPs when they make purchase decisions.

As stated, the initial cost of most assets is relatively easy to determine. It's the purchase price. LCC really comes into effect when the operating costs of assets need to be calculated. If available, historical asset cost records are an invaluable source of information for making initial LCC projections. If asset cost records are not maintained, cost data may be available from other NPs or vendors for making LCC estimates. Vendor information needs to be used with caution, however, as the data may be biased to show the lowest cost projections.

Two analytical techniques that can be used to predict annual operating costs are analogy and parametric estimations. The specific method selected depends on the cost behavior being analyzed and the asset selection phase. For example, as the project moves from a conceptual phase to its actual selection, the cost data and performance criteria for the asset become more clearly defined. As a result, the cost projection technique can change.

With analogy methods, an old asset similar to the new one is chosen for analysis. Once the annual operating costs of the old system are collected, they are adjusted to account for dissimilarities in operating the old and new assets. The adjustment is illustrated for the cost of material as follows:

Old system materials cost = $450 per month

New system materials cost = $450 x 1.10 = $495

The estimation indicates the cost of materials in the new system is expected to be 10 percent higher than in the old system or $495 rather than $450. The increase may occur due to using more costly material, a higher level of operational use, or a combination of the two factors. In analogy estimating, a straightforward percentage adjustment is made to the historical costs in the old system.

Analogy estimation is especially useful in the early phases of the asset selection and when the least amount of cost information is known. It is a useful technique because it is simple to apply, but it is subject to the limitation that the results are strongly influenced by the opinion of the individual making the estimate. As a result, projections may result in a wide range of estimates.

Another cost projection technique is called the parametric method. This method uses a mathematical equation called a parametric equation that relates an asset's performance characteristics to its costs.[4] A linear relationship is assumed to exist between the operating costs and the performance characteristics of an asset. A linear cost equation is formulated by analyzing the relationship between the past changes in costs and new performance requirements. The estimated energy cost of new heating equipment can serve as an illustration of this technique, assuming there is a linear relationship between the total cost of electricity used in new heating equipment and the amount of power consumed per hour (the British thermal unit [Btu] rating), the number of hours the equipment is operated per year, and the cost of electricity per watt-hour. This relationship lends itself to the following formulation.

Total cost of power consumption = Btu rating x annual operating hours x cost of power per watt-hour

Today there is an increased level of awareness among NP organizations regarding carbon footprints and green issues. With this equation, the cost of energy consumption can be compared among several potential equipment purchases, thereby allowing the organization to reduce its carbon footprint. It may become apparent that a higher purchase price is justified because a "green" asset performs its tasks more efficiently, which results in lower total energy costs over the life of the asset. Without such comparisons, the NP is jumping into a financial hole as it finds its operating costs continuing to increase while it faces new budget cuts.

IMPLEMENTING LCC MANAGEMENT: TWO EXAMPLES

Traditional asset selection methods review the purchase price of a new asset and compare it with the budget appropriation. If the purchase price is less than the appropriation, the asset is considered acceptable for purchase. Usually little consideration is given to the effect of the asset purchase on the NP's future operating costs. The result can create an unanticipated and continually growing cost of operations. LCC provides the potential for keeping those costs in check and the NP out of a financial hole. The approach is called LCC management.

LCC management can serve as an asset cost management system both before and after a purchase is made. The acceptance of an LCC approach as a managerial tool requires the full support of top-level management. It requires the use of LCC management reports for each asset purchased and an understanding of both the benefits and limitations of this analysis. The use of LCC management does not mean the asset with the lowest total cycle cost is always purchased, but it does mean the reasons for selecting an alternative with higher costs must be justified. The next section of the chapter illustrates two examples of this management technique.

Making an LCC Comparison: Vehicles

The first step in using LCC management is to design an LCC report for selecting assets. Figure 10.1 illustrates such a report—the asset selection form. Under LCC management, a report of life-cycle costs is required for every asset purchased. In figure 10.1, the asset selection form is used to evaluate the purchase choices between two new vehicles.

In the vehicle selection form, costs are separated into purchase price, maintenance costs, and fuel expenses. These costs are shown as totals over the five years the vehicle will be used. Maintenance costs are usually available from automobile dealers. Total operating costs are equal to the total of these three costs reduced by the estimated vehicle trade-in values. Once the total life-cycle costs are computed, the average cost of operating the vehicles over their estimated five-year lives are shown along with their operating costs per mile.

The purchase price difference between the two vehicles is $13,000. The small SUV is less expensive than the electric vehicle. Today there is a push to reduce every organization's carbon footprint, but such reductions may result in increased operating costs. If these cost effects are not recognized, the NP has committed itself to a series of expenditures that may not be sustainable if its annual appropriations are reduced.

FIGURE 10.1
LCC Report for Vehicle Selection

LCC REPORT: Vehicle Selection

VEHICLE CHOICE:	SMALL SUV	GAS/ELECTRIC
Number of miles per year	20,000	20,000
Total purchase price	$25,000	$38,000
Total maintenance costs: (tires, oil changes, scheduled maintenance)	3,725	3,125
Total fuel costs	8,140*	11,300**
Less: Trade-in value	(1,000)	(2,500)
Total Operating Cost over 5 years	$35,865	$49,925
Average cost per year	$7,173	$9,985
5-year cost per mile (100,000)	$0.36	$0.50

* Assuming a $2.85 per gallon for gas; 35 miles per gallon on the SUV

** Assuming a $2.85 per gallon for gas; 75 miles per gallon on the e-car; battery recharging every 40 miles and a $2 cost per recharge.

> ASSET RECOMMENDED FOR PURCHASE AND JUSTIFICATION: The total operating cost of the e-vehicle is approximately $15,000 more than the small SUV over the five-year life of the two vehicles. It is recommended that the small SUV should be purchased. If a $15,000 grant is available for purchasing e-vehicles, then the gas/electric vehicle should be considered as a potentially viable alternative.

In figure 10.1, maintenance costs are composed of oil changes, tire purchases, and scheduled dealer maintenance. The dollar costs are shown for the entire five years, not annually. It is assumed the SUV's maintenance expenditures are $600 higher than are the e-vehicle's maintenance costs. The e-vehicle is assumed to have better mileage than the SUV, but it will also need battery recharging every forty miles or 500 recharges per year. The cost of recharging the e-vehicle's batteries must be added to its annual operating costs causing its total fuel costs to be higher. The e-vehicle has a higher trade-in value, but this cash flow does not make up for the increased fuel costs.

With this analysis, it can be seen that unless the NP can receive a "green" grant of about $15,000, it should buy the small SUV. Without a grant, the NP will be using a larger portion of its appropriations for operating the e-vehicle and reducing its funding for value-added activities. In figure 10.1, there is a management section at the bottom of the form, Asset Recommended for Purchase and Justification, which summarizes the results of the LCC analysis. The summary provides a quick rundown of the outcome of the report.

In the example, it is assumed that both vehicles have a life of five years. If it can be shown that one of the vehicles has a longer life than the other, the LCC analysis needs to take such a change into account. It is also assumed that both vehicles have the capacity to serve the needs of the NP such as hauling load, inside space criteria, and so forth.

GO GREEN

State Takes Steps to Turn Fleet Green

Buzz Powell, Auburn Test Track Manager, says "Often times these vehicles have to be purchased at a slightly more initial purchase price, but if they deliver a much lower life cycle cost then it's a better investment for the taxpayers."[5]

Making an LCC Comparison: Lighting

One continuing operating cost for an NP organization that is not often considered as a life-cycle cost is facility lighting. The cost of electricity for the NP can be substantial over a long period, and the organization cannot operate without the incurrence of this utility cost. Therefore, it is important to consider how it can be reduced. As an example, consider the LCC effects of replacing incandescent lights with energy efficient lighting. Figure 10.2 illustrates a LCC calculation comparing one energy efficient light with a comparable number of incandescent lights.

In this example, the two lighting choices have different lives: 760 vs. 10,000 hours. Ten thousand hours are equivalent to around 14 months of constant use. Using this information and the additional information in figure 10.2, it is possible to determine the LCC of the two alternatives. In making the calculation, it must be realized that it will take thirteen incandescent bulbs to be used for every one fluorescent bulb replaced (10,000/760 = 13), and each time an incandescent bulb is replaced there is a labor cost attached to that activity. The replacement cost for incandescent and energy efficient lighting is $4.75 and $3.00 respectively. Although the cost of electricity for the lighting alternatives is the same ($0.10 per KWh), the incandescent bulb has a higher wattage (60 vs. 15) as well as a shorter life.

The calculations in figure 10.2 show the difference in cost over a comparable life cycle is $90.00. This means it costs $90 more to use a set of equivalent incandescent bulbs for 10,000 hours than an energy efficient light. When the total number of incandescent lights in a building is multiplied by $90, it can be seen that the long-term savings is substantial. Such savings allow the NP to redirect saved monies to patron value-added activities. At the

FIGURE 10.2

LCC Report for Electricity Costs: Lighting

The following information has been collected about both types of lighting:

LIGHTING CHOICE:	INCANDESCENT	ENERGY EFFICIENT
Life in hours	760	10,000
Purchase price	$2.00	$15.00
Cost to replace*	$4.75	$ 3.00
Cost per kWh**	$0.10	$ 0.10
Light wattage usage	60 watts per hour	15 watts per hour

  * Replacement costs include the ordering costs, the cost of custodians replacing the bulbs, and inventory carrying costs of storage and damage.

** Energy guide information is attached to many consumer products, such as air conditioners. This information provides estimates of the annual energy cost of operating such equipment. Cost data are provided based on hours of yearly use translated into kilowatt-hours (kWh).

LCC REPORT: LIGHTING CHOICES

The following report outlines LCC over 10,000 hours of usage for one energy efficient bulb as compared with an equivalent number of incandescent bulbs.

	LIGHTING CHOICE:	INCANDESCENT*	ENERGY EFFICIENT
1. Purchase Cost		$ 2.00	$15.00
2. Operating cost per kWh			
a. Incandescent: (.76 kWh life x 60 watts x $0.10 per kWh) x 13		59.00	
b. Energy Efficient: (10 kWh life x 15 watts x $0.10per kWh) x 1			15.00
3. Replacement cost over 10,000 hours			
a. Incandescent:	$4.75 x 13	62.00	
b. Energy Efficient:	$3.00 x 1		3.00
Total life-cycle cost		$123.00	$33.00

* The numbers are rounded

ASSET RECOMMENDED FOR PURCHASE AND JUSTIFICATION: The total operating cost of one energy efficient light is $33 compared with an equivalent number of incandescent lights of $123. Each energy efficient light will create a savings of $90 over the 10,000 hours of usage. Ten thousand hours of usage are equivalent to using the energy efficient light about 14 months, twenty-four hours a day. It is recommended that the incandescent lighting be replaced with energy efficient lighting as the incandescent lights burn out.

bottom of the report in figure 10.2, Asset Recommended for Purchase and Justification, a recommendation is made to replace the incandescent bulbs.

Although the initial cost for the energy efficient bulb is more than seven times higher, it incurs lower costs over its life cycle. Most budgets only allow for a specific line item allocation for expenditures such as supplies, thus creating the conditions for a financial hole in the NP's future operating costs. Unfortunately, long-term savings in an annual budget is not a focus for managers who are trying to have their annual budget approved. Long-term savings will not become an important managerial concern until LCC management is adopted within an NP.

DEVELOPING A POLICY OF NP LIFE-CYCLE MANAGEMENT

Successful financial performance does not automatically translate into satisfactory patron service or employee development. Therefore, managerial performance should be viewed with a wider perspective than just financial issues. LCC management does this by going beyond prepurchase analysis to the evaluation of results.

LCC management is concerned with comparing the initially projected costs with the actual costs incurred and reviewing the factors that cause projected costs to change. LCC management is used as a long-term management tool. LCC analysis is a useful technique for asset selection. By itself, it provides managers with a structured way of analyzing asset choices. But, LCC management must take LCC analysis one step further, to post-purchase review.

LCC management incorporates long-term cost control over assets. Therefore, LCC analysis is only the first step in asset cost control. Follow-up procedures must be in place to ensure the cost projections were made with reasonable accuracy. If significant deviations occur, the reasons for those cost variances need to be determined. LCC management uses actual post-purchase cost information to evaluate a manager's initial LCC analysis. If there are significant cost variances, managers need to explain why costs have significantly changed from projections. Depending on the difference between initial LCC projections and currently incurred costs, it may be necessary to make renewed cost projections based on new data. If the new projections show that costs cannot be controlled, it may be necessary to consider the abandonment of an asset prior to the end of its useful life as a last resort to curtail accelerating or uncontrollable operating costs.

Table 10.1 illustrates a cost report that can be prepared on a yearly basis to evaluate the accuracy of LCC projections. In table 10.1, the report is prepared using the data for the small SUV from figure 10.1. The report is prepared after the vehicle was in use for one year. The report is developed as a cumulative cost report accumulating costs over the life of the SUV. For example, in year 2, it would record a two-year summary of cost data. In table 10.1, actual costs are compared with the SUV's projected costs to evaluate their accuracy.

There are three basic aspects to the management report in table 10.1. The headings show LCC projected costs in column two which are compared with actual costs in column three. The last two rows show the number of miles driven and the cost of fuel, respectively. Any significant variances in the report need to be analyzed in detail. The manager who developed and approved the original LCC estimates will need to explain large deviations from projections. By analyzing significant variances, the operating cost of an asset can be better controlled. Aspects of a manager's performance evaluation should be related to this report. If the reasons for cost overruns are not reasonable, the variances should reflect negatively on a manager's annual performance evaluation.

In reviewing this report, it is immediately apparent that the number of miles driven is less than the 20,000-mile projection. At the estimate rate of $2.85 per gallon cost originally

TABLE 10.1
Annual review report comparing LCC projected and actual operating costs

ANNUAL REVIEW

VEHICLE: SMALL SUV

(1) ANNUAL OPERATING COSTS	(2) ANNUAL LCC PROJECTED COSTS	(3) ACTUAL ANNUAL COSTS	(4) VARIANCE*
Maintenance	$ 745	$ 750	$ (5)
Fuel charges	1,628	1,457	171
Total annual operating cost or *variance*	$2,373	$2,464	*$165*
Number of miles	20,000	17,000	
Fuel Cost Per gallon	$2.85	$3.00**	

* Unfavorable amounts in parentheses
** Average cost per gallon during the year

projected in figure 10.1, the three thousand miles of reduced mileage should have reduced fuel costs by $244 (3,000/35 x $2.85). This effect was countered by the increase in the cost of gas per gallon of $0.15 or a total of $73 ($3.00 $2.85 x 17,000). Therefore, fuel charges were only reduced by $171 ($244 - $73). It is important to separate a cost variance into its two components—miles driven and cost of fuel. Such discrepancies need to be investigated as they can reveal important information about the LCC projections. In this case, the variances can be traced to the increased cost of gasoline per gallon and a reduction in the number of miles the car was driven. With any discrepancy, the LCC projections should be reviewed to determine if managers intentionally introduced bias into the analysis in order to skew the results toward a specific choice. This does not appear to be the case in this example. Finally, it should be noted that in table 10.1 results show a total overall favorable variance on the SUV's use of $165 in its first year of operation.

Depending on the LCC analysis, downtime may influence the reason operating costs of an asset vary from original LCC projections. For example, downtime measures could include the time to repair the vehicle after a breakdown. Downtime might be a significant contributor to the increase in per-unit cost of a system. If the electric vehicle had been purchased instead of the SUV, downtime might relate to the time devoted to recharging the batteries before the vehicle was available for use.

SUMMARY

LCC techniques expand upon the traditional methods for making purchasing decisions that match an appropriation with the purchase price of an asset. LCC analysis requires consideration of factors that are usually given little emphasis under traditional asset selection methods. LCC management expands LCC analysis into the formal NP decision making process. It requires follow-up procedures to determine if the projected benefits from the assets actually materialized. The primary objective of LCC performance evaluation is to determine how well asset life-cycle costs are being controlled. It is one thing to predict costs and base asset selections on these predictions, but after the purchase date, costs must be monitored and efforts taken to keep them in line with projections. When cost projections have a high level of uncertainty, variances from projected levels may be acceptable. Evaluations of manager's performance should take such factors into account.

As an NP purchases assets, it has to ensure that it is not building in high operational costs to maintain these new assets. With a high level of operating costs and reduced budget appropriations, the NP may be faced with reducing its value creating activities or even shutting its doors. Those NPs have slowly fallen down a financial hole.

NOTES

1. Present value concepts assume that there is a time value to money and that $1 received today is worth more than if it is received tomorrow or one month from today because money received today can be invested and interest can be earned on that investment. The importance of the time value of money concept is that it allows cash flows made in different time periods to be made comparable. It is difficult to make managerial decisions about the purchase and the cost of operating assets without the ability to make cash flows in different time periods comparable. The time value of money concept allows comparisons to be made as to whether cash outflows today or in the future are more costly to the organization. By just simply comparing the total dollar amounts, this determination cannot be made.

2. In the typical accounting system, the costs of supplies used in a new asset, for example, are combined with the costs of all annual supply expenses; therefore, it is difficult to separate the operating costs related to specific equipment.

3. "APA Releases Life-Cycle Cost Software," ForConstructionPros.com, June 4, 2010, www.forconstructionpros.com/online/Asphalt-News/APA-Releases-Life-Cycle-Cost -Software/41FCP16432.

4. Estimating costs with parametric equations can become very complex. It is possible to use regression analysis in parametric estimation of operating costs. An equation of this nature is based on historical data and used to predict cost levels for a new asset. Such an equation would be as follows:

$$\text{Total cost} = A + B(x) + C(y) + D(z) + \text{systemic error (I)}$$

5. In this equation, x, y, and z are elements that represent factors computed through the mathematics of regression analysis. The elements B, C, and D represent real data, such as the Btu rating, that influence the total cost. The element A represents a constant.

Lisa Blackwell, "State Takes Steps to Turn Fleet Green," WNCFTV.com, June 10, 2010, www.wncftv.com/localnews/96098704.html.

ELEVEN

RELEVANT OR NOT, HERE WE COME

Opportunity cost is a key to decision making and a concept of which a good manager should always be mindful.

Mark Vaughn

Total costs are not important when alternative cost choices are being made. Although it may sound surprising, using total costs can lead a manager into another financial hole. If total costs are not important in making a good managerial decision, then what is important? The costs that are important in making financial decisions are relevant, sunk, and opportunity costs. These costs are not accumulated within an NP's financial reporting system. They are costs that are not calculated by the NP's bookkeeper. The NP's manager needs to be able to explain to the bookkeeper or even their accountant the analysis they want developed; otherwise they will receive a total cost report. The reader of this chapter will understand how to ensure that viable decisions are made using these three cost concepts.

DIFFERENTIAL COSTS

The costs that differ between two alternative decisions are called differential costs (DC). Such costs are important in identifying the best alternative among several choices. DCs are sometimes called incremental costs. These costs are the dollar differences of alternative future actions that can be taken by a manager. For example, if the purchase prices of two vehicles are $10,800 and $10,000, the DC is $800. If the cost of license plates for each vehicle is $75, this is not a DC because the charge is the same. Therefore, the cost of license plates should not be a consideration in determining which of the two vehicles to purchase. If total costs were compared, $10,875 would be compared with $10,075. With budget restrictions in effect, the decision is to purchase the $10,075 vehicle, but most decisions are not this simple, as will become apparent shortly.

When an NP decides to make a change in the manner it delivers its services, as for example when outsourcing is being considered, it is important to clearly identify the relevant costs related to the change. Such a process begins with the identification of the specific services being considered for outsourcing. Do released employees provide services that go beyond their department functions? If so, will those functions have to be separately funded once a department is eliminated? After those service areas are completely identified, it is necessary to calculate the total outsourcing costs to compare with the projected savings from outsourcing these services. If there are any costs involved in making these changes, they, too, must be taken into consideration as differential costs in the transition. These are the basic considerations that need to be taken into account when such an organizational change is being considered.

> ### SO YOU WANT TO WALK ON MY RUG!
>
> Bunnell can keep its city offices at Flagler County headquarters for another two years, although it may have to pitch in more money. Commissioner Alan Peterson said he wanted Bunnell to pay any incremental costs of the city using space in the county's Government Service Building. Some of the incremental costs commissioners discussed were wear on carpeting and janitorial services.[1]

Consider the decision to close a sub-office of an NP organization as another example of differential cost analysis. The costs of operating the office are shown in table 11.1. The total cost of operating the branch is $36,500, and initially it may appear that this is the amount saved if the branch is closed (i.e., the total costs).

However, to determine the actual amount of savings that will occur if the branch is closed the differential costs of operating the branch need to be separated from the total costs. The salary of an administrator is allocated to this branch based on the time spent assisting with branch functions. As shown in table 11.1, $6,500 of the administrator's salary is allocated to the branch. The administrator would not be released if the branch were closed; therefore, the administrator's salary is not saved by the closing. A technician working at the branch who receives a salary of $10,000 would be laid off if the branch were closed. Utility charges would be saved when the branch was closed. There will be a $9,000 saving in rent payments and approximately one-half of supplies still have to be purchased, creating only a $4,000

TABLE 11.1
Total costs and differential costs for an NP sub-office

COST ITEM	TOTAL COSTS	DIFFERENTIAL COSTS
Administrative salary	$ 6,500	—
Technician wages	10,000	$10,000
Utility charges	3,000	3,000
Annual rent payments	9,000	9,000
Supplies	8,000	4,000
Totals	$36,500	$26,000

savings. The DC savings from closing the branch are $26,000—the costs that change as a result of closing the branch, not the total costs of operating the branch. Table 11.1 shows that the cost savings from closing the branch are less than the branch's full operating cost—costs of $10,500 will continue to be incurred regardless of whether the branch is closed ($36,500—$26,000). These costs are unavoidable and should not enter into the decision-making process. It may also become apparent that by closing the branch, clients are now using the main office more and therefore those costs are likely to increase as a result of the branch closing. Only costs that will differ as a result of alternative future choices—the DCs (positive and negative)—should be allowed to influence managerial decision making.

DIFFERENTIAL COST ANALYSIS

The application of differential costs to decision-making problems is called differential cost analysis (DCA). DCA is similar to life-cycle costing (LCC) in that it is concerned with the cash flows. But, it differs from LCC analysis because DCA is concerned with the cost differences between two alternative choices, not the total operating costs over their lives. DCA can be used in conjunction with LCC analysis. Once the least-cost asset is chosen with LCC, the costs of operating that new asset can then be compared with the costs of operating the old asset to be replaced in order to determine if a replacement is a cost-effective decision.

Examples of DCA use are:

- Whether to develop a new asset within the NP or purchase it from an outside vendor
- Deciding on new equipment alternatives
- Deciding to outsource services
- Identifying the mixture of resources allocated to various projects
- Change in NP policies

When using DCA, only the cash flow differences between alternatives are analyzed. The financial reports that assign expenses to various fiscal periods are not part of DCA as it is very difficult to identify the cash flow from these reports. Differential costs are the costs that will change because of selecting one decision alternative over another, and this information is not reported on the financial statements.

A cost that does not affect DCA is sunk costs. Sunk costs are costs that cannot be changed, and for that reason, they are not part of a DCA. Examples of these costs are depreciation, long-term contract payments, scheduled debt payments, and liability insurance payments. Identifying these costs will allow them to be separated from those costs that influence managerial decisions. As an example of a sunk cost, consider the calculation of depreciation. Depreciation expense is calculated by assigning the cost of an asset to the time periods in which the asset is used. Although the future amount to be paid for an asset is an important consideration in decision making, after the purchase price has been paid, its accounting disposition is of little importance to managerial decision making. The yearly depreciation charges based on the price paid for an asset years ago are not useful for future decision making. For this reason, the sunk cost or purchase price of an asset acquired yesterday has no bearing on the decision to replace it today. Most managerial decision-making questions are future oriented, and historical cost allocations have no effect on those decisions.

From a personal view, people make incorrect decisions based on sunk costs. If you have invested $4,500 into fixing up an old car and you decide to keep investing in the car because you already have $4,500 into repairs, you are making a decision based on your sunk costs.

Those are the costs that you cannot change, and they should not be the deciding factor in making the decision to continue to repair a vehicle. If you have decided to repair the vehicle due to sentimentally attached to the car, then you are making a decision based on a different criteria. Gamblers and stock market investors often make decisions based on sunk costs. Gamblers continue to bet based on the amount they have already lost. Investors continue to buy the stock to average down their per share investment cost in a company.

DCA requires caution when determining which costs change when considering alternatives. Variable costs will change among alternatives but fixed costs can also change. For example, a decision may result in the elimination of a fixed cost, such as the fixed salary of an administrator if that administrator's position is eliminated. Therefore, no assumptions should be made about the changeability of variable and fixed costs until the nature of alternatives is fully understood. Further the costs alternatives include a number of estimates that may be biased in one direction or the other. Many of these estimates provided by that manager may be difficult to verify. The degree of bias introduced into these estimates is difficult to isolate because evaluative information is usually not collected for making after-the-fact comparisons with original estimates.

Two brief examples of DCA are presented here. The first one, illustrated in table 11.2, deals with choosing between developing a computer program using NP employees or purchasing the software from a vendor. The second example, in table 11.3, deals with the decision to replace an aging asset.

SOFTWARE CHOICES

In table 11.2, the cash cost of developing customized software is compared with the cash cost of purchasing it, and the difference, which is the cost saving or loss from purchase, is shown in the last column, "Difference." The costs of developing the software are listed under the heading "Computer resources." These costs include the costs of computer time, supplies, and the estimated cost of using other assets that were purchased due to software development activities within the NP. The cost of salaries assigned to the software development team is based on the actual time incurred, and these costs are shown as direct labor in table 11.2.

TABLE 11.2
Analyzing the decision to purchase software from a vendor or developing it internally

ITEM	DEVELOPMENTAL COSTS	PURCHASE COST	DIFFERENCE
Computer resources	$ 40,000	—	$ 40,000
Direct labor	80,000	—	80,000
Allocated overhead	—	—	—
Purchase price	—	$200,000	(200,000)
Debugging costs	—	15,000	(15,000)
Totals	$120,000	$215,000	$(95,000)

This illustration assumes that any software maintenance costs are insignificant.

Labor costs are related to the activities—such as writing and debugging programs—that are required to complete the system and get it up and running.

Direct labor costs may not be differential costs because they would be incurred anyway. If the personnel assigned to the software project are taken away from these other tasks and not replaced, the NP still incurs the same labor costs. Those labor costs are not differential costs, nor part of the development costs. If these labor costs are related to hiring additional workers to replace staff assigned to the computer project, then the costs of the new hires are differential costs. Labor costs must be carefully analyzed to determine if they are differential costs. In the illustration, it is assumed that the labor costs are differential costs.

The internal software developmental costs need to be compared with the cash cost of purchasing the software, which is equal to the purchase price and the vendor's charges for debugging the software. The start-up costs of labor time and training are classified as "debugging" costs in table 11.2. These costs are incurred by the NP not the vendor.

The differential cost is $95,000, meaning the NP would save $95,000 if it developed the software with its own resources and personnel, assuming all estimates of the cost of internal development are accurate. This also assumes that the quality of the customized software and the vendor purchased software are the same. DCA indicates that the best choice is to develop customized software.

The item titled "Allocated overhead" is shown in table 11.2 with zero balances. Only actual cash out-of-pocket costs related to the alternatives are included in the DCA. Any overhead costs allocated to software development will still remain unchanged in the NP whether or not the software is developed internally; therefore, overhead is not a differential cost. Of course, future incurrence of additional overhead due to internal development activities is part of the DCA.

TOO HOT TO HANDLE?

Table 11.3 provides another example of DCA used to decide whether an old furnace should be replaced. The illustration in table 11.3 represents the cash flows arising from the decision to trade in an old furnace for a new energy efficient furnace. The old furnace is still working. The cash cost of operating the new furnace over its estimated twenty-year life and the cash cost of operating the old furnace over its remaining estimated life of ten years is shown in

TABLE 11.3
Analyzing the decision to replace a furnace

CASH ITEM	OLD FURNACE	NEW FURNACE	DIFFERENCE
Operating cost outlay*	$400,000	$275,000	$125,000
Equipment depreciation	—	—	—
Disposal value of old	—	(2,000)	2,000
Cost of new furnace	—	35,000	(35,000)
Disposal value of new	—	(3,500)	3,500
Totals	$400,000	$304,500	$ 95,500

*Assumes a 10-year period for the old furnace and a 20-year period for the new furnace.

the first row of table 11.3. These are historic ten- and twenty-year estimates about operating costs, which assume that these costs will not change—that fuel costs will remain constant, for example. Today, with rolling blackouts of electricity in some areas and continually changing fuel prices, this may not be an accurate assumption.

The operating costs in the example include fuel and maintenance and repair costs but not depreciation. To emphasize that depreciation is not part of this calculation, the second item in the first column is listed as depreciation and left without a dollar balance. Depreciation is considered a sunk cost and does not affect the decision to purchase or not to purchase a new asset. The third item in the first column is the current disposal or salvage value of the old asset. The $2,000 salvage value is deducted from the cash outlays for the new furnace, reducing the total cash paid out to replace the old furnace. If the old furnace is not replaced, at the end of its life it will have a disposal value of zero. The cost of the new furnace is shown in the fourth row, and $3,500 is the estimated salvage value that will be received for the new furnace at the end of its twenty-year useful life. This amount is also deducted because it is a reduction of the total cash outlays for the new furnace.

The "Difference" column shows that purchasing the new asset will save $95,500. This column records the relevant costs associated with purchasing or not purchasing the new furnace. It should be noted that the useful lives of the two assets are different and longer than one year. In such a case, the time value of money would affect the decision to purchase the new furnace. Many illustrations overlook the difference in assets' lives by assuming that the old asset will have the same remaining useful life as that of the new asset, which tends to equalize the cash flows. The assumption of equal lives for new and old assets is an oversimplification. It is uncommon in actual practice to find a new asset with the same remaining life as the older asset it is replacing.[2]

Another difficulty with relevant cost analysis is the quality of the data. Data may be incorrect or purposely biased. A technique called sensitivity analysis can help to overcome such problems. Sensitivity analysis is a method that allows variations in the data. For example, if the fixed costs in a break-even calculation are biased low, it is possible to recalculate the equation with higher fixed costs to show how "sensitive" the break-even point is to the biased data. Sensitivity analysis shows how sensitive the final solution is to possible errors in the data. Sensitivity analysis can incorporate a number of additional "what-if" scenarios into the data. This approach is useful if the quality of the data is suspect or if a number of different scenarios have an equal chance of occurrence. For example, in table 11.3 the operating cost of the new furnace is $275,000, but if this cost is biased because of a favorable estimate provided by a vendor, the analysis should be recalculated. Additional what-if calculations could be related to changes in the estimated useful lives of the furnaces. Numerous what-if calculations can be added to the analysis to help overcome some of the difficulties caused by biased or incorrect data.

LET'S INCORPORATE OPPORTUNITY COSTS

Another relevant cost that needs to be taken into account is opportunity costs. An opportunity cost is the value attributed to the next best alternative that was foregone because of a decision. For example, if money is taken out of the bank to purchase an asset, it no longer receives the interest it was earning in the bank. The lost interest is considered an opportunity cost and needs to be taken into account as managerial decisions are made. When a university decides to stop operating its university bookstore and sell it to a commercial company, the opportunity cost is the lost profits it received from operating the bookstore. Opportunity costs are not recorded in the financial statements, but if they are not incorporated into the managerial decision process, incorrect decisions are likely to be made. From a personal perspective, a student who sits in a classroom while a lecture is delivered also is incurring an opportunity cost. The opportunity cost is the cost of the lost wages he could have earned from a job during the time period he was in the classroom taking notes.

> ## LET'S GO TO SCHOOL
>
> When there's an economic downturn, everybody wants to go back to school, because the opportunity cost is quite low. If you don't have a job, you might as well be in school.[3]

Outsourcing the Check Out

With the technology available today, it is possible to outsource the book checkout system from librarians at the circulation desk to self-service kiosks. The automated kiosks include electromagnetic theft detection systems to prevent patrons from passing the kiosks without checking out their books. A barcode or RFID chip in books, CDs, and DVDs is read at the kiosk, integrated into the library's book records, and a printout provided to the patron showing when the book needs to be returned. The system provides statistical usage reports for library staff and remote access for staff and patrons. Up to 90 percent of library materials can be checked out using this automated system. Such automated systems can cost upward of $200,000. Should the checkout process be automated?

Table 11.4 provides an illustration of the costs involved in making the decision including opportunity costs. It can be seen that the cash outlay for the automated checkout system is $220,000. There are very little internal savings from purchasing the automated system. If two librarians are not reassigned, they are no longer needed as their functions have been automated. The labor savings from releasing these two librarians is $75,000. The reduced salary is a savings that occurs from implementing an automated system, but there are no other savings. The purchase price does not include training for library staff. Therefore, the library will have to spend $8,000 in training costs. No major upgrades would be needed on the system for the next five years. In addition, an opportunity cost of $25,000 is recognized in table 11.4. It is assumed that the monies for the system were taken out of accounts on which the library had earned interest. Interest on the $220,000 for the next five years would

TABLE 11.4
Analysis for automating circulation checkout procedures

CASH ITEM	OLD SYSTEM	NEW SYSTEM	DIFFERENCE
Operating cost outlay*	$ —	$220,000	$(220,000)
Labor savings*	75,000	—	75,000
Training personnel	—	8,000	(8,000)
Opportunity cost	—	25,000	(25,000)
Totals	$75,000	$252,000	$ 178,000

*Two circulation librarians will be terminated

be $25,000. If the purchase is completed, the library will no longer receive these discretionary monies. For that reason, opportunity costs need to be incorporated into the analysis. As currently illustrated, the automated system will cost the library $178,000. Each NP organization needs to perform an analysis that shows the differential cost of each purchase. Afterwards, based on this analysis, the staff can decide whether they believe the purchase is a worthwhile choice.

If the library received a grant specifically designated for the entire purchase of the automated system, this would completely change the analysis and make it a more viable choice. Under these conditions, the labor savings of $75,000 would pay for the $8,000 worth of training and the library would have a net savings of $68,000 by purchasing the system instead of a $178,000 outlay as in the previous example.

Regardless of the choice made by an NP, they should take the effect of any opportunity costs into account. For decision making, this is a real cost that helps to outline the true effect of any managerial decision. Yet caution needs to be exercised when the word "opportunity cost" is used. Decisions should not be based on nebulous visions of opportunity costs that may never occur. For example, arguments can be set forth that if an NP builds a unique and expensive building, tourists will come along with a flow of tourist dollars. Thus if we do not build the structure, there is a lost opportunity (e.g., tourist dollars). Many cost projections incorporate opportunities such as these that are highly unlikely to materialize. Care needs to be exercised as such reports are reviewed.

SUMMARY

Distinctions between differential, sunk, and opportunity costs are important in managerial decision making. Differential or incremental costs allow the manager to focus on those costs that are really important to the outcome (opportunity costs) or unimportant (sunk costs). It is important to know why sunk costs need to be ignored even though they may seem important to a decision. Furthermore, the manager needs to be able to identify those opportunity costs that affect a decision. All sorts of decisions require the correct identification of these costs. Decisions related to purchasing equipment, implementing new policies, dropping or increasing patron services, hiring outside services, and replacing facilities are examples of decisions based around differential, sunk, and opportunity costs. NP decision makers need to avoid financial holes and maintain financial viability. The method explained in this chapter helps them make good financial decisions for their organization.

NOTES

1. Frank Fernandez, "Bunnell May Keep Offices in County Headquarters—at a Cost," *Daytona Beach News Journal*, June 23, 2013, www.news-journalonline.com/news/local/flagler/2010/06/23/bunnell -may-keep-offices-in-flagler—at-a-cost.html.

2. For examples using present value in this analysis see G. Stevenson Smith, *Managerial Accounting for Libraries and Other Not-for-Profit Organizations* (Chicago: American Library Association, 2002).

3. Mitchell Hartman, "A Jobless Recovery and Lost Generation," *Marketplace*, June 18, 2010, http:// marketplace.publicradio.org/display/web/2010/06/18/mm-a-jobless-recovery-and-a-lost-generation.

APPENDIX
ESSEX UNIVERSITY LIBRARY

One of the first steps in helping the director of Essex University Library and the head of the ILL work with activity-based accounting methods is to determine the salary and mailing costs that are related to ILL activities.

ASSIGNING SALARY EXPENDITURES TO ILL ACTIVITIES

Based on the information provided in the problem, the following schedule shows a method of salary allocation to the ILL.

	ILL	NON-ILL
Librarian's salary—$45,000	$27,000 (60%)	$18,000 (40%)
Staff salary—$47,000	42,300 (90%)	4,700 (10%)
Totals	$69,300	$22,700

Salary costs related to ILL activities are $69,300.

ASSIGNING MAILING EXPENDITURES TO INTERNAL AND EXTERNAL FUNCTIONS

A second step would be to determine how the mailing expenditures are as–signed to various activities in the ILL. Mailing costs are divided between inter-nal requests from patrons at our Essex University and requests from external libraries for our materials on a 70/30 split. Using that information, it can be determined that the mailings costs of $35,000 are divided between external and internal requests as follows:

$35,000 x .70 = $24,500 internal requests from our patrons

$35,000 x .30 = $10,500 external library requests for our materials

The head of the ILL has provided a list of activities that are performed within the ILL, but she has not assigned any times required to perform the activities. If the number of minutes for each activity were known, it would be possible to determine costs on a worked-minute basis.

Without any information on work minutes, it is still possible to assign sal-ary and mailing costs to the number of books and articles processed through the ILL based on activities. The following costs provide a method to allocate these costs to book and article processing activities.

MAILING EXPENDITURES AND ACTIVITIES

1. Internal Requests from Our Patrons: Assigned Mailing Costs: $24,500

The mailing costs are all assigned to books and articles using the following ratios tied to mailing activities; as the head of ILL has not time-weighted these activities, each activity is given an equal weight:

ACTIVITY	WEIGHT
Mailing request for article	1
Mailing request for *book*	1
Mailing *book* back after loan period	1
	3

Using the schedule, it can be seen that two activities are related to books and one is related to articles. For this reason, the ratios used to allocate costs are 2/3 and 1/3 as follows:

Books	2/3 x $24,500 =	$16,333
Articles	1/3 x $24,500 =	8,167
Total		$24,500

2. External Requests for Our Materials: Assigned Mailing Costs: $10,500

ACTIVITY	WEIGHT
Mailing out article to requesting library	1
Mailing out book to requesting library	1
	2

Using the schedule, it can be seen that the activities are equally divided between books and articles. For this reason, the ratios used to allocate costs are ½ and ½ as follows:

Books	½ x $10,500 =	$ 5,250
Articles	½ x $10,500 =	5,250
Total		$10,250

The total estimated costs for mailing books is $21,583 ($16,333 + $5,250) and total mailing cost for articles is $13,417 ($8,167 + $5,250).

SALARY EXPENDITURES AND ACTIVITIES

Now the question arises as to how to assign the salary expenditures of $69,700 to the processing of books and articles. When all the activities are reviewed, it can be seen that some activities relate to both the processing of books and articles whereas other activities are only related to books or articles. For example, photocopying articles for external requests is only performed for article requests. The only way to classify these activities into internal and external activities is by giving them an equal weight. Therefore, the number of activities that are performed, for either external or internal requests are counted and classified. Although it would be better to assign activity weights on minutes worked, pages copied, or other similar measures, this information is currently not available.

1. Internal Requesting Activities
   a. Both (6)

      Check current collection for books
      Check current collection for journals
      Mail request to loaning library
      Check receipt of item
      Notify patron
      Record pickup by patron

   b. Books, only (3)

      Receive returned book from patron
      Follow-up on nonreturn
      Return book to loaning library

2. External Requesting Activities:
   a. Both (2)

      Mail out book or article request
      Collect fee on loaned materials

   b. Books, only (5)

      Locate book
      Document loaned material
      Check returned loaned materials
      Record returned book
      Reshelf book

   c. Articles, only (1)

      Photocopying article

MATRIX OF ACTIVITIES

	BOTH	BOOKS	ARTICLES
Internal from our patrons	6	3	0
External for our materials	2	5	1
Totals	8	8	1 = 17 total activities

Total Salary Costs $69,300/17 = $4,076.47 salary cost per activity

Salary costs of $69,300 are assigned to common activities (both), books, and articles using a rate of $4,076.47 per unit. For example Internal Books is computed by multiplying three from the above Matrix of Activities table times $4,076.47 which equals **$12,229**.

	BOTH	BOOKS	ARTICLES	TOTAL
Internal	$24,459	**$12,229**	0	$36,688
External	8,153	20,382	$4,076	32,611
Totals	$32,612	$32,611	$4,076	$69,299

The outcome of the review of activities, as related to books and articles, results in the following cost assignments to Internal and External Requesting Activities.

1. Total Costs Related to Internal Requesting Activities

A. TOTAL COST

	BOTH	BOOKS	ARTICLES	TOTAL
Mailing	$ 0	$16,333	$8,167	$24,500
Salary	24,459	12,229	0	36,688
Totals	$24,459	$28,562	$8,167	$61,188

The ILL has information about usage statistics. The average number of internal (9,750: books, 6,000 and articles, 3,750) and external requests (5,500: books 4,500 and articles 1,000) along with data on the average number of articles and articles requested by these groups.

B. PER UNIT COST

		$ TOTAL/UNITS
Both	$24,459/9,750 =	$2.51
Books	$28,562/6,000 =	$4.76
Articles	$8,167/3,750 =	$2.18

2. Total Cost Related to External Requesting Activities

A. TOTAL COST

	BOTH	BOOKS	ARTICLES	TOTAL
Mailing	$ 0	$ 5,250	$5,250	$10,500
Salary	8,153	20,382	4,076	32,611
Totals	$8,153	$25,632	$9,326	$43,111

B. PER UNIT COST

		$ TOTAL/UNITS
Both	$8,153/5,500 =	$1.48
Books	$25,632/4,500 =	$5.70
Articles	$9,326/1,000 =	$9.33

PER UNIT COST OF INTERNAL AND EXTERNAL ACTIVITIES

REQUEST AREA	BOTH	BOOKS	ARTICLES
Internal	$2.51	$4.76	$2.18
External	$1.48	$5.70	$9.33
Totals	$3.99	$10.46	$11.51

SUMMARY

The results of the activity analysis have raised a lot of questions. The most expensive area appears to be external requests for articles at $9.33 per request. It also becomes apparent that the cost of article requests is much higher than external requests for books on a per unit basis. In addition, there is a relatively high cost for serving book requests from our patrons at $4.76 per book. The director and Alice are surprised to see such a large dollar difference in per unit costs as it was always thought the servicing of external book and article requests had the same costs.

The director and the head of ILL would like to reduce or combine activities in order to reduce costs but not the quality of the services. The director would also like to know how to better assign the costs of activities related to "both" internal and external requests to a specific ILL activity. The table showing per unit costs does not assign any clear responsibility for these costs in column two "Both."

At this point, the director has requested Alice to conduct a survey of employees to determine the time that they spend on the various departmental activities that have been identified. It is hoped that through a more detailed investigation of activities, it might be possible to curtail activities that are not really contributing value to the department's services.

Comment: The traditional financial reports that are prepared for the library do provide information that allows the director to be able to control or reduce costs in a logical manner. These generalized financial reports are prepared for reporting to the library's external funding agencies and library board members. They are not prepared for managerial decision making. For this reason, they are often ignored by library managers who use "burn-the-building" cost-cutting measures instead of the surgical methods required to allow the NP to maintain the greatest level of service to patrons during a budget crisis.

GLOSSARY

Accrual method of accounting   An accounting method that focuses primarily on the passage of time to recognize revenues and expenses rather than on the flow of resources or cash.

Activity-based costing (ABC)   A system of costing that uses detailed identification of activities as a way to trace costs to services and products. It, like traditional-based costing, uses allocations to assign costs to cost objects, but it uses a more detailed analysis of activities or cost drivers.

Allocation   A method of assigning costs, usually overhead, to cost objects to determine their full costs. Overhead is assigned using a surrogate to assign the costs. Commonly used surrogates or cost drivers are direct labor, number of personnel, or floor space, for example.

Analysis of variance   The determination of the difference between actual costs and standard costs (established as projections before the activity began) to evaluate performance. If actual costs are less than the standard established, the variance is favorable. If the actual costs are more than the standard costs, the variance is unfavorable.

Appropriations   An appropriation is a legal authorization for making expenditures within set dollar amounts, time periods, and specified purpose.

Assets   Items with a determinable future value and that are owned by the organization.

Balanced scorecard   A method to evaluate progress toward strategic initiatives that coordinates objectives, performance measures, and targets for meeting the organization's long-term mission. The balanced scorecard does not simply measure financial targets. It combines financial targets with patron, internal processes, and learning and growth targets to achieve a more holistic view of the organization's progress.

Book value   The book value of an asset is the asset's net value. Book value is determined by deducting all the accumulated depreciation recorded on an asset from its purchase price.

Break-even analysis (Cost-Volume-Profit analysis)   A methodology that identifies the point, in total units or dollars, where the total revenues exactly equal the total costs of a profit-generating activity.

Budget   An annual planning tool used to match financial resources with financial expenditures. The budget provides a means to achieve the organization's stated mission.

Cash basis of accounting   A method of accounting that only records business transactions when a cash exchange has occurred. It emphasizes the flow of cash rather than the passage of time or the flow of resources for transaction recognition.

Contracts for performance   These are agreements between higher-level administrators (HLA) and the organization. The contract is signed prior to the HLA accepting a new position. It provides contractual terms upon which the HLA will be evaluated after a specified time period. Failure to live up to the agreed-upon terms can result in termination or reassignment.

Contribution margin   The contribution margin is the difference between the selling price and the variable costs of a unit. It measures the per-unit contribution to profit or the reduction of total fixed costs.

Controllable cost   A controllable cost is one that can be influenced by the decisions made by a manager. Thus, the cost is defined as controllable.

Cost driver   A cost driver is the activity that causes costs to increase over time.

Cost object   A cost object is an activity or project upon which the cost analysis is focused and consequently upon which costs are separately accumulated and reported.

Deferred maintenance   If maintenance expenditures are not made on a routine basis to keep the organization's fixed assets in proper working order, the maintenance has been deferred. As a result, the service potential of the asset has been reduced. The gap between the maintenance performed and maintenance required to keep the asset in proper working order can be measured and recorded, and it is called deferred maintenance.

Depreciation   The allocation of the purchase price of a long-term fixed asset to the time periods to which the asset provides benefits. Depreciation is the accounting recognition of the usage or obsolescence of the asset. It is recorded as an expense, but unlike other expenses, it does not create a cash or resource outflow.

Differential cost   The costs that differ between two alternatives are known as differential costs. Differential costs are important for choosing between alternatives. Sometimes differential costs are called marginal costs.

Direct cost   Those costs such as direct labor and direct materials that can be easily traced to a cost-generating project or activity.

Direct method of cost allocation   A method of cost allocation whereby the cost of all support departments are directly allocated to producing departments in order to determine the full cost of the producing departments. The direct method does not use allocations and reallocations of costs to determine the full costs as is done in the step-down method of cost allocation.

Discounted cash flow   This is a methodology that takes into account the cash flows generated by an activity or project within the context of present value analysis. It allows for the comparability of cash flows among alternative choices where the cash flows are of differing amounts and are realized over different time periods.

Discretionary cost   Although discretionary costs can be variable, fixed, or mixed, their distinguishing characteristic is that they are incurred at the discretion of higher-level managers in the organization. These costs may be expended for additional staff training, for example.

Encumbrance   An encumbrance discloses a commitment of budgetary monies for an anticipated purchase. It is recorded at the time the purchase order is issued by the organization. An encumbrance is not a liability.

Expenditure   Expended resource outflows during the current period. Expenditures include most expenses.

Expense   Expiration of resources, or the incurrence of a liability recognized by the passage of time, or the incurrence of the actual expenditure used to generate revenues and provide services in the current period.

Financial Accounting Standards Board (FASB)   This is the accounting body that sets accounting principles, rules, and standards that are to be used in accrual accounting.

Fiscal period   A twelve-month period used in tabulating financial reports. A calendar period is from January to December, but a fiscal period may be any twelve-month time period. Most government organizations in the United States use a fiscal period from July to June.

Fixed cost   Total fixed costs stay constant over increasing volume levels and per-unit fixed costs decrease as volume or units increase. An example of a fixed cost is a supervisor's salary.

Flexible budget   A budget whose dollar allocations change as the volume level, such as number of patrons, upon which it is based increases or decreases. A static budget's dollar allocations remain constant regardless of the level of volume changes.

Full cost   The full cost of a project or activity includes all the direct costs such as direct labor and direct materials, as well as an allocation for overhead.

Generally accepted accounting principles (GAAP)   The principles, standards, and interpretations that are followed, used, and accepted in preparing financial statements.

Governmental Accounting Standards Board (GASB)   This is the accounting body that sets the accounting principles, rules, and standards that are to be followed by state governments.

Historical cost   The original purchase price of an asset is its historical cost.

Indirect cost   Another term used to describe overhead costs. *See* Overhead.

Inventory   Amounts such as supplies that are held in storage and not yet used but classified separately from other long-lived assets because of their shorter-term nature.

Life-cycle costs   After an asset is purchased, costs continue to be generated by that asset over its entire life. These costs include maintenance expenditures, for example. When all such costs are considered, they are called the life-cycle costs of the asset.

Life-cycle management   A method of asset selection and decision making that is closely tied to the total life-cycle cost of the asset being purchased.

Long-lived assets   Assets that have a life over one year or longer than the current fiscal period. Such assets are usually equipment or property.

Market value   This is the price at which an asset will sell in an open market. With many assets, this is difficult to determine. Market value is also called fair market value.

Mission statement   Organizations develop a mission statement for guiding their employees toward a unified vision. The method in which the mission is integrated into an organization can vary from none to incorporating it into the daily activities of each employee.

Mixed cost   A mixed cost is one that has the attributes of both variable and fixed costs.

Noncontrollable cost   Costs that cannot be controlled by a specific manager at their hierarchical level in the organization are considered to be noncontrollable costs. At a higher organizational level in the organization, these costs may be controllable. *See* Controllable cost.

Nonfinancial performance measures   Many performance measures are developed from financial reports and budgets. When other sources of information are used for the development of performance measures, such as surveys, they are called nonfinancial performance measures.

Nontraceable costs   With some overhead costs, the cost-benefit relationship in finding a cost driver that causes the incurrence of these overhead costs is not worth the effort to identify the relationship. Additionally, the relationship may be so tenuous as to not be meaningful. These costs are considered to be nontraceable costs.

Non-value-added activity   Activities that are performed that add no value to the outcome of a task. For example, waiting is not a value-added activity. Such wait times may occur during committee meetings that add little or no direct value to the quality of patron services.

Opportunity cost   This is the cost of the next best alternative. It is not a cost that is recorded in the accounting records, but it is a cost that influences decision-making choices.

Original cost The purchase price of an asset is referred to as its original cost.

Overhead These costs are associated with the general activities of the organization and must be incurred but are difficult to identify directly to a specific activity. These costs are the opposite of direct costs, which are closely associated with a project or activity. Under activity-based costing, the objective is to reduce overhead costs to a smaller percentage of the total costs of operations.

Relevant range The range of normal operations within the break-even curves. It is the unit range the organization has operated within before. It helps to provide assurances that costs will behave linearly within the range and the cost relationships will remain consistent.

Responsibility accounting A system of performance evaluation that assigns cost control responsibility to a specific functional manager in the library. The manager is responsible for costs at the point where they are incurred in the organization. Responsibility accounting provides for more detailed control at the point of cost incurrence rather than later as costs are accumulated in the financial reports.

Revenues Amounts that are realized or owed as earned. The definition of "earned" can vary with the method of accounting being used.

Salvage value The estimated value remaining in an asset at the end of its useful life. This is the estimated price at which an asset can be sold when it is retired.

Sensitivity analysis Sensitivity analysis has applications to many situations. It is applied to a set of data relationships by varying one factor and then another to determine how sensitive the factors are in changing the project outcomes.

Standard cost Costs that are preset at efficient levels within attainable limits. These costs are set to achieve cost control over cost-incurring processes. They can be used as an evaluation of managerial performance in achieving the standards.

Strategic planning Strategic plans are long-term plans for organizational activities. Strategic plans are more difficult to achieve than operational plans because they occur in a time horizon of one year and beyond.

Sunk costs Costs that continue regardless of the managerial decision that is made. For example, the price paid for an asset and in some cases directors' salaries are considered sunk costs. These costs should not be a factor in managerial decision making.

Value-added activity Value-added activities refer to those functions that add value to the direct outcome of an activity. Time spent increasing the quality of an outcome is a value-added activity. Not all activities add value to a process.

Value gains Value gains relate to higher-level administrator contributions to the long-term decision-making process as determined by employee surveys. If the higher-level administrators' contribution adds to the value of the decision-making process as reflected in the final outcome of the decision, it is referred to as value gains.

Variable cost Total variable costs increase over increasing volume levels and per-unit fixed costs remain constant as volume or units increases. An example of a variable cost is direct materials such as supplies.

Variance Variances record the difference between two sets of numbers. In accounting, variances record the difference between budgeted dollars and the actual spending, for example. The reporting of variances shows how closely actual spending conformed with projected spending. Thus, variances provide evaluations on managerial performance.

INDEX

NOTE: *f* following page numbers indicates figures and *t* indicates tables.

You may also be interested in

WINNING LIBRARY GRANTS
A GAME PLAN

Herbert B. Landau

Whether you're a newbie taking on the process for the first time or an experienced administrator looking to shore up finances, this book will help you find the dollars your library needs.

PRINT: 978-0-8389-1047-4
EBOOK: 7400-0474
PRINT/EBOOK BUNDLE: 7700-0474
184 PGS / 6" × 9"

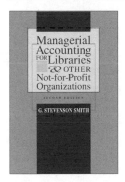

MANAGERIAL ACCOUNTING FOR LIBRARIES AND OTHER NOT-FOR-PROFIT ORGANIZATIONS, 2E
G. STEVENSON SMITH
ISBN: 978-0-8389-0820-4

THE FRUGAL LIBRARIAN
EDITED BY CAROL SMALLWOOD
ISBN: 978-0-8389-1075-7

THE ALA BIG BOOK OF LIBRARY GRANT MONEY, 8E
EDITED BY ANN KEPLER
ISBN: 978-0-8389-1058-0

MOVING MATERIALS
EDITED BY VALERIE HORTON AND BRUCE SMITH
ISBN: 978-0-8389-1001-6

INTERLIBRARY LOAN PRACTICES HANDBOOK, 3E
EDITED BY CHERIÉ L. WEIBLE & KAREN L. JANKE
ISBN: 978-0-8389-1081-8

MANAGING LIBRARY VOLUNTEERS, 2E
PRESTON DRIGGERS AND EILEEN DUMAS
ISBN: 978-0-8389-1064-1

Order today at **alastore.ala.org** or **866-746-7252!**
ALA Store purchases fund advocacy, awareness, and accreditation programs for library professionals worldwide.